Meeting the Needs of Students with Limited or Interrupted Schooling: A Guide for Educators

Meeting the Needs of Students with Limited or Interrupted Schooling: A Guide for Educators

Andrea DeCapua

William Smathers

Lixing Frank Tang

Ann Arbor
THE UNIVERSITY OF MICHIGAN PRESS

ISBN-13: 978-0-472-03351-5

2012   2011   2010   2009   4   3   2   1

Preface

Meeting the Needs of Students with Limited or Interrupted Schooling: A Guide for Educators represents our combined experience observing classrooms and schools; interacting extensively with teachers, students, administrators, and program developers; and participating in numerous national and regional conferences with focus groups and seminars on the diverse types of English language learners (ELLs). For more than five years, we have concentrated on students with limited or interrupted formal education (SLIFE) enrolled in secondary schools; during this time, we became keenly aware of the unique challenges that this particular student population poses. Our experiences and observations have led to this book, which offers suggestions that we believe will help educators struggling to meet the needs of these students as they help them adjust to the new culture and a new educational experience.

This book is not theoretically grounded, although we do refer to some methods that have come from various theories of second language acquisition. It is not supported by data accumulated over an extended period of time. Requisites of this nature would require the undertaking of a long-term, broad-based academic study or studies with a national focus on the shifting demographics of immigrant student populations in U.S. high schools. The field has yet to produce such a scholarly work. What we offer, instead, is a guide featuring practical suggestions for teachers, administrators, program developers, and others who are concerned for the academic success of SLIFE. The suggestions are based on actual observed practices that address specific SLIFE issues and offer solutions.

Those of us who have worked in the field of English as a second language (ESL) or teaching English to speakers of other languages (TESOL) know that there are many theories that deal with the fascinating topic of post-adolescent second language acquisition. It is not our intention here to deal with theoretical issues. Theories of post-adolescent second language acquisition have generated a variety of recognizable classroom practices used in ESL classrooms today. While these have proven to be pedagogically sound practices, the principle that underlies these practices is founded on the assumption that ESL students already possess a level of literacy and an accumulated base of academic knowledge in their first language that facilitates the transfer of these skills to the U.S. high school classroom. In fact, studies have shown that students who do possess these requisite skills in their native or first language not only make the transfer to English-based instruction but tend to do better academically than monolingual English language students. For SLIFE, assumptions of this sort simply cannot be made.

We found that nearly all schools place SLIFE in an age-appropriate grade level regardless of their language or academic skills. Most SLIFE are placed in regular ESL or bilingual classes where such exist; if there are no ESL or bilingual classes, they are placed in mainstream classes with their American peers. Whichever the case, it is a disservice to these particular students, as the standards and practices in these classes are, at least initially, beyond their abilities. They lack the basics assumed in these classes. Countless teachers, administrators, and others approached us after presentations at conferences and seminars to ask us what they can do to help these students because regular classroom activities do not work and the academic clock is ticking. The problem is widespread. The high drop-out rate among SLIFE and long-term ELLs is indicative of the failure of schools to offer realistic alternative academic programs that address the needs of these particular students. We must work together to find viable programs that will help these individuals make the transition to a new culture and become productive, contributing citizens of it.

We owe a sincere debt of gratitude to the many teachers who invited us into their SLIFE classrooms, introduced us to their genuinely amazing students, and took time out from their busy schedules to talk with us and answer our many questions. We would also like to thank the many school administrators, district supervisors, curriculum specialists, and others who opened the doors that enabled us to observe classes, examine materials, and conduct inquiries.

Acknowledgments

Grateful acknowledgment is made to the following authors, publishers, and individuals for permission to reprint previously published materials.

Omniglot.com website for Akkadian cuneiform (www.omniglot.com/writing/akkadian.htm) on page 25. Website copyright Simon Ager. Used with permission.

Pearson Education, Inc., for material from Maslow, Abraham H., *Motivation and Personality*, 3d ed. Copyright © 1987, pages 15–31. Adapted and used with permission of Pearson Education, Upper Saddle River, NJ.

Students who allowed their materials to be used.

Every effort has been made to contact the copyright holders for permission to reprint borrowed material. We regret any oversights that may have occurred and will rectify them in future printings of this book.

Contents

Chapter 1

Who Are SLIFE?

I've been in this school district for 32 years. I grew up in this area, and I'm telling you, I've never seen anything like this. It's always been an Irish, blue-collar, working-class type of town, with a few African-American families. Then about three years ago, we got a family from Mexico, and well, we now have a lot of Spanish-speaking kids who've never really gone to school. We really don't know what to do with them. The ESL teacher tries really hard, but these students don't have the schooling to be in high school, but they have to come here because of their ages.

—Principal, suburban high school

USERS OF THIS TEXT WILL, NO DOUBT, BE WELL AWARE OF THE EXTRAORDINARY INCREASE IN THE immigrant population in the United States over the past decade and the resultant changing face of the school population. Data from the U.S. Census Bureau's Current Population Survey of March 2007 revealed a record 37.9 million immigrants, both legal and illegal, meaning that one out of every eight U.S. residents is now an immigrant. Of these nearly 38 million immigrants, 10.8 million are school-age children, who account for almost all the increases in public school enrollment across the country. Among these 10.8 million children, those who are ELLs more than doubled between 1989–1990 and 2004–2005 (NCELA, 2005).

Unlike previous immigration trends, which saw large numbers of immigrants settling primarily in major urban areas, the current trend indicates widespread immigration across the nation, with large new immigrant populations moving to smaller urban centers as well as to large urban areas and to rural and suburban areas. Rural areas of the Southeastern and Midwestern states have seen especially significant increases in recently arrived immigrants and are struggling to cope with the needs of school-age children who have not yet developed proficiency in English and who increasingly come from backgrounds with less formal schooling (Capps et al., 2005; Johnson, 2005; Kandel & Cromartie, 2004). From 1993–1994 to 2004–2005, Alabama, Kentucky, Nebraska, and Tennessee experienced increases of more than 300 percent in their K–12

ELL populations; South Carolina's was more than 700 percent, and Nevada's more than 200 percent (NCELA, 2005). In Utah, while total growth in the student population is below the national average, the growth in ELLs has been more than double that of the national rate (Hosp & Mulder, 2003).[1]

As the number of ELLs increases, so too does the subpopulation of ELLs who have limited or interrupted formal schooling and whose schooling is not on par with the grade-level expectations of the U.S. public school system. This subpopulation may have experienced interrupted schooling due to war, migration, lack of educational facilities, cultural dictates, or other circumstances; they may have had limited access to schools in their home country, or their schools may have lacked highly trained teachers and/or educational resources. For some of these ELLs, high school may be their first exposure to literacy in any form. In addition to facing academic challenges, many in this subpopulation have to deal with emotional traumas, such as fleeing civil wars or natural disasters or who may now be separated from immediate family.

Exactly how one should refer to this particular group of students is still open to debate and there is no single accepted label to identify this subpopulation. In the literature, they are referred to by various labels, such as "LFS ELLs" (Limited Formal Schooling ELLs) (Freeman & Freeman, 2003); "unschooled migrant youth" (e.g., Morse, 1997); "newcomers" (e.g., Constantino & Lavadenz, 1993; Short, 2002); "migrant youth" (e.g., Nava, Hernandez, Rubalcava, & Palacios, 1995); and "SIFE" (Students with Interrupted/Inadequate Formal Education, e.g., DeCapua, Smathers, & Tang, 2007; New York State Department of Education). The acronym SIFE has been increasingly used throughout the United States by organizations such as NABE (National Association of Bilingual Educators) and is the official term for this subpopulation in New York State.

In this book, we have chosen to modify the acronym SIFE because we believe this label does not accurately reflect the reality of many of these students, for instance, those whose education may never have been "interrupted" (DeCapua et al., 2007). The educational systems of some students' home countries may not have provided the same opportunities for learning, and/or the requirements and expectations may have been vastly different from those of the U.S. system; or students may never have even been enrolled in formal schooling prior to their arrivals in the United States. We therefore propose the term SLIFE, students with limited or interrupted formal education, which we believe is a more accurate label.

Challenges and Issues for SLIFE

Students with limited or interrupted formal education bring with them a broad, highly variant range of challenges; nowhere is this more evident than at the high school level where the overall drop-out rate of all ELLs is alarmingly high (Morse, 1997; Osterling, 2001; Tienda & Mitchell, 2006). Although accurate drop-out numbers are nearly

---

[1]   For detailed statistics, visit the U.S. Department of Education's Office of English Language Acquisition, Language Enhancement and Academic Achievement for Limited English Proficient Students (OELA) at www.ncela.gwu.edu/policy/states/index.htm.

impossible to obtain and assess for a host of reasons (Barton, 2005; National Center for Education Statistics, 2005; National Governors' Association, 2005; Valenzuela, Fuller, & Vasquez-Heilig, 2006), it has been claimed that ELLs account for one-quarter of the high school drop-out rate of which an alarming, although not altogether surprising, 70 percent are SLIFE (Fry, 2005).

The challenges facing high school ELLs are much greater than those facing native speakers, given that ELLs must both learn English and develop the requisite academic knowledge in a language not their own in order to graduate. SLIFE, however, face especially formidable challenges. These students not only need to develop cognitively demanding grade-level academic language proficiency while learning grade-level content knowledge, but they must also confront the additional challenges of developing basic literacy and numeracy skills and acquiring basic academic knowledge, all within the relatively short time frame of secondary school (DeCapua et al., 2007). Furthermore, the implementation of the 2002 No Child Left Behind (NCLB) Act, the federal law holding schools accountable for the academic performance of all children, requires high-stakes testing for which SLIFE tend to be ill-prepared.

The mandates set forth in NCLB have created additional challenges for SLIFE. In order to comply with the NCLB mandates, many states in the United States now require high school exit exams in English language arts (commonly reading and writing skills), math, history, and/or the sciences. These exit exams are categorized as "high-stakes tests" because high school students must pass these tests in addition to earning a specified number of credits in a variety of disciplines in order to graduate from high school with a recognized diploma.

Four of the largest states with high percentages of ELLs have instituted the passing of exit exams as a requisite for a high school diploma. As of 2006, California began requiring all students to pass the California High School Exit Exam (CAHSEE) in order to earn a high school diploma. The CAHSEE, created by Educational Testing Services (ETS), assesses reading, writing, and math skills. Texas mandates a satisfactory performance on the Texas Assessment of Knowledge and Skills (TAKS) at Grade 11 as a prerequisite to obtaining a high school diploma. The TAKS tests students in English language arts, mathematics, social studies, and science. The state of Florida has established the Florida Comprehensive Assessment Test (FCAT), measuring reading and mathematics skills. Florida students must obtain satisfactory results on the FCAT by Grade 12 in order to obtain a high school diploma. In New York State, students are required to take the New York State Regents Exams in English language arts, mathematics, global history and geography, U.S. history and government, and sciences. As all these various exit exams assume that those taking them have native or near-native fluency in English, strong literacy skills, numeracy and/or content-knowledge, these tests are frequently seen as posing insurmountable obstacles for SLIFE.

Faced with learning English literacy skills and the academic knowledge required by cross-discipline testing, SLIFE often become frustrated with the academic requirements for graduation and drop out at alarming rates. SLIFE need additional help if they are to remain in school and achieve academic success.

This book attempts to address some of the many issues facing SLIFE, beginning with the correct identification of SLIFE, many of whom are not being properly identified or tracked such that this population often gets lost in the system. SLIFE frequently find that they have been placed with other ELLs and/or in an age-appropriate mainstream class without the requisite support for their additional needs. Too often they do not receive the extra expertise, time, and help that they require. Teachers—even ESL teachers—frequently lack adequate training because this population has specific literacy development and content-area knowledge needs that are markedly different from other ELLs. There is also a lack of textbooks and materials specifically designed for these students at the secondary level. Furthermore, most schools do not offer a clear support structure with teachers, guidance counselors, parent coordinators, social workers, and the families all involved. Finally, there is a lack of in-depth proven research on what works with SLIFE. These are just some of the more salient variables associated with this student population, and schools serving them must take into account this wide range of issues affecting the performance of these students.

WHO ARE SLIFE? SUMMARY CHART

- Lack basic academic skills and concepts, content knowledge, and critical-thinking skills and may not be literate in their native languages
- Confront the triple challenges of learning English and becoming proficient in a pre-scribed body of knowledge and skills, while simultaneously preparing for high-stakes testing
- Have limited time to accomplish all of this successfully in order to graduate from secondary school

---

Identifying SLIFE

Of central concern to all schools should be the accurate identification of SLIFE. In addition to wanting to provide the best services possible, accurate identification of this population should be treated as a priority because it has an impact on account-ability and has repercussions for school funding issues, as well as the rights of parents and students. Accurate identification of potential candidates for SLIFE programs often poses major challenges, including being able to determine

- levels and/or quality of prior education
- native language literacy abilities
- levels of English proficiency
- the cultural values associated with education in the home countries

In the most extreme examples, such as students entering high school with little or no literacy in their native languages, identification is relatively easy. In reality, however, most cases are not always so immediately clear. For example, SLIFE may appear to have completed the requisite number of school years in their home countries yet lack sufficient academic content knowledge and literacy skills to graduate from high school in the United States. The educational resources and/or the education standards previously available to them may not have permitted SLIFE to attain the academic knowledge and higher-level thinking skills necessary for success in U.S. schools. Schools may have lacked sufficient resources, whether well-trained teachers, textbooks, libraries, lab equipment, or even desks and writing implements. Classroom procedures may have focused primarily on rote learning or memorization, or may have concentrated on passing national tests and exams. Some SLIFE come from schools where they were not surrounded by print and where advanced reading and writing skills are not high priorities.

> In my country I go school everyday but no books, no pens. Only teacher have. Teachers says, we say. Teacher write, we write. Not like here.
>
> —Kareem

SLIFE may have found it necessary to absent themselves from school regularly in order to help with seasonal labor, take care of family members, or for other reasons.

> If my mother need help, I stay home because she have to go work. I'm the eldest so I have to help my brothers and sometimes my mother or cousin she need me.
>
> —Ines

In educational systems where students must provide their own materials, they may have lacked the funds necessary for books, writing materials, and other basics, and thus may not have been able to complete required work. All of these factors contribute to inadequate schooling to meet the requirements and standards for successful completion of and graduation from U.S. high schools.

> Everywhere I go, I see words, not like in my country. My brother go school but you have to buy everything and too expensive.
>
> —Alpha

> My home, it is in the country. School very different, we have no building, it's open. We have book, but old and you have to buy so sometimes we share so we don't have to buy. Can't do homework if don't have book, but these expensive.
>
> —Armando

Possible Indicators

Because SLIFE come from such disparate backgrounds, there are various indicators to be considered in attempts to "flag" a student as a potential SLIFE. Any one or a combination of the indicators listed could indicate the need to evaluate an ELL more carefully.

POSSIBLE INDICATORS
• Inadequate school records, no school records, or school records with gaps
• Reports by student and/or parent/guardian of not having attended school
• Poor attendance records from prior schools, frequent absences, and/or tardiness at current school
• Low literacy level in the native language
• Weak grasp of grade-level content material

Although weak school performance is most often determined by reading and mathematics proficiency, performance in other academic subjects such as science and social studies should also be taken into account. The vocabulary and concepts for such disciplines are difficult for all ELLs (Echevarria, Vogt, & Short, 2008; Gomez & Madda, 2005) but especially so for SLIFE who lack foundational academic knowledge. The checklist on page 7 can be used to help educators and administrators in initially identifying potential SLIFE.

Checklist for Identifying Potential SLIFE

Student's Name _____

Evaluator _____

Interpreter's Name _____

Date of Evaluation _____

1. _____ English is not the primary language of the home.

2. _____ came to the U.S. after Grade 2

3. _____ upon enrollment, has had at least two years less schooling than peers

4. _____ functions at least two years below expected grade level in reading

5. _____ functions at least two years below expected grade level in math

6. _____ is pre-literate in native language

7. _____ low literacy level in the native language

8. _____ lack of complete educational records

9. _____ Parent/guardian reports student has missed schooling.

10. _____ poor attendance records from prior schools

11. _____ consistent absences in the current school

12. _____ consistent lateness in the current school

13. _____ poor grades

14. _____ weak grasp of academic content

15. _____ limited experiences in content area classes in English

16. _____ poor performance on standardized tests

Additional Instruments for the Identification of SLIFE

ADDITIONAL VERIFICATION INSTRUMENTS
• Standardized tests such as 　▪ the *Comprehensive English Language Learning Assessment* (CELLA) from Educational Testing Services (ETS) 　▪ the *Stanford English Language Proficiency Test* (SELP) from Harcourt Assessment • State tests such as 　▪ the *New York State English as a Second Language Achievement Test* (NYSESLAT) 　▪ the *California English Language Development Test* (CELDT) 　▪ the *Texas English Language Proficiency Assessment System* (TELPAS). • Student writing samples in L1 (native language) and/or in English • In-depth student interviews • Interviews with parents or completion of questionnaires if parents are literate and comfortable with questionnaires and are willing to fill them out

Tests

Once SLIFE have been at least tentatively identified, multiple instruments should be used to gain a more complete picture of students' literacy and academic knowledge (Mace-Matluck, Alexander-Kasparik, & Queen, 1998; Ruiz-de-Velasco & Fix, 2000). English language proficiency tests are generally used to identify which students are ELLs in order to place them in appropriate classes and to offer appropriate support services. Some states have their own standardized English language proficiency tests; other states use a variety of commercially available tests.[2] These language proficiency tests are not designed to assess ELLs' literacy, numeracy, or academic knowledge; but they may help teachers pinpoint specific areas of English that need additional work and/or support, such as the correct use of verb tenses, sentence structure, and comprehension difficulties, as well as others.

Because standardized tests in subject areas are generally not available in languages other than Spanish—and even in Spanish few are available—it may be difficult to use these in identifying SLIFE with low levels of English proficiency. Another pitfall of overdependence on standardized tests is that poor performance on standardized tests may be a language issue rather than a knowledge issue, or it may possibly be due to lack of familiarity with how to negotiate the test, such as filling in the bubbles on a Scantron answer sheet.

---

[2] A list of states and the English language proficiency tests used is available at www.ncela.gwu.edu/expert/faq/25_tests.

Regardless of the assessment instrument(s) chosen, care must be taken that only one instrument is used across school populations. If, for instance, SELP is used for seventh graders and NYSESLAT is used for eighth graders, there is no standard basis for comparison. Likewise, if different schools in a school district use a different assessment instrument for the same grade, there is no standard basis for comparison.

Writing Samples

For SLIFE with some basic literacy, production of a writing sample, either in their native languages and/or in English, can provide some indication as to their level of literacy and English proficiency. Students at low levels of proficiency may be assessed by asking them to describe a series of pictures; somewhat more proficient students may be asked to choose one topic on which to write from a list of topics. In order to assure an accurate assessment of the native language production of more proficient students, the school community should have access to the services of a person who is proficient in that language and qualified to evaluate writing and other language production.

Writing prompts may consist of a series of pictures for students to describe, like those shown in Figure 1, or some clip art images can be put together for students to write about.

FIGURE 1:   Sample Writing Prompts

Parent/Guardian Interviews

Even when records of prior schooling in the home country are available, additional issues may frequently arise. Parents/guardians are not likely to be aware of their rights and the rights of their children with regard to education and may be extremely sensitive to possible accusations that they neglected the education of their children. They may also fear that their children will not be accepted at the U.S. school if there are gaps in the records or if they indicate poor performance. Parents, guardians, and/or children, wanting to appear to have age-appropriate schooling, may report more years of school than were actually completed. Consequently, at times, school documents may have been fabricated or tampered with to give the illusion of a full, age-appropriate educational background.

Once an ELL has been identified as a possible SLIFE, the school should arrange for an interview with the student's parent(s)/guardian(s) to provide them with as much information as possible about what it means to be identified as a SLIFE and the services/programs this entitles the student to receive. Interviews, usually more so than written documents, can provide insights into where and with whom students lived prior to immigration. This information can indicate potentially significant factors in determining the nature of students' prior educational experiences. Students may have moved frequently and may not have had opportunities to attend school consistently; others may have lived in refugee camps with few or no schooling opportunities (Crandall, Bernacvhe, & Prager, 1998; Fishman & Monroe, 1990). The residual effects of separation from family members, homesickness, and of living in transitional areas for extended periods of time may affect their school behaviors and their abilities to concentrate and learn (Apfel & Simon, 1996; Suárez-Orozco, 1989; Trueba, Jacobs, & Kirton, 1990; Zhou & Bankston, 2000). These and other affective factors (see Chapter 3) are potentially significant in determining the nature of their prior educational experiences (Fishman & Monroe, 1990; Hones & Cha, 1999).

Because many parents/guardians feel uncomfortable and intimidated by schools and school personnel, an atmosphere of trust must be established either before or during interviews. Gaps in school attendance are often due to sensitive matters; parents/guardians may be embarrassed, distressed, or feel threatened if they sense in any way that they are being censured or blamed for the lack of complete school records or their children's incomplete prior educational experiences. Thus, creating an informal dialogue generally elicits more information than conducting formal, structured interviews.

When interviewing parents or guardians, every effort should be made to locate the interview at the school because conducting it at school presents several advantages.

- It provides the parent/guardian with the opportunity to meet more people involved in the student's learning activities.

- It provides an opportunity to take the parent/guardian and student on an informal tour of the school's facilities, which is more relaxed than sitting in an office.

- Parents/guardians are more likely to ask specific questions during these tours.

- It may offer parents/guardians and students a chance to meet and talk with other students in the school from similar backgrounds.

In all interviews, the school's parent coordinator(s) should be involved to serve as a critical link between the school and the parents (see Chapter 7). If the student and parent(s)/guardian(s) are not proficient in English, then the interview should be conducted in the native language with an appropriate interpreter whenever possible. In instances where the parent coordinator is bilingual, he or she may assist with interpretation and translation. Although securing the services of a qualified interpreter may pose a problem in areas with traditionally low numbers of immigrant populations and/or for students who possess varying degrees of literacy skills in languages less commonly spoken in the United States, such as Urdu or Somali, every attempt should be made to do so through both formal and informal (e.g., religious or community associations) channels. Parents/guardians with little proficiency in English and without the benefit of interpreters will not understand, or may misunderstand, the information that school personnel are trying to convey (Trueba, Jacobs, & Kirton, 1990).

In interviews with parents/guardians and students present, the school should avoid having the student act as interpreter, particularly for sensitive matters or issues that may be beyond the student's cognitive state of development. Furthermore, having the student translate may place the child and parents/guardians in inappropriate and uncomfortable roles that may be at odds with cultural expectations (Kratochvil, 2001).

The school community should be aware that not just any speaker of the same language will necessarily suffice. If the interpreter speaks a different variety of the native language, as is often the case with Spanish or Arabic for example, the interpreter needs to be aware of different terminology and nuances of meaning. For example, if the interpreter speaks Mexican Spanish and the student speaks Venezuelan or Dominican Spanish, is the interpreter aware of possible areas of misunderstanding? In addition, children and their families need to trust the interpreter. If the interpreter is a person of different social status or family connections, will the SLIFE family be open in their communication or will they hesitate to share personal information? Will the family feel the interpreter can be trusted to keep the meeting confidential?

While the quality of prior education is not always easy to determine, well-planned interviews with appropriate interpreters as needed can help teachers and administrators explore the nature of educational experiences that SLIFE may have had prior to entering a U.S. school. The questions provided on page 12 are intended for use as a guide when conducting interviews to elicit as much information as possible. These questions should be used to open the door to past educational experiences and will, in all probability, need to be modified depending on the language proficiency of those involved in the discussion. Ideally, the teachers and/or administrators involved in the discussion of past educational experience will see these questions as a springboard to opening a dialogue or discussion that allows participants to tell the story of their past school experiences.

Student Interviews

Students are often the most valuable source of information regarding their educational experiences because interviews with them can potentially produce valuable information about their academic backgrounds. Factors to keep in mind when interviewing ELLs who have been tentatively identified as SLIFE are listed on page 13.

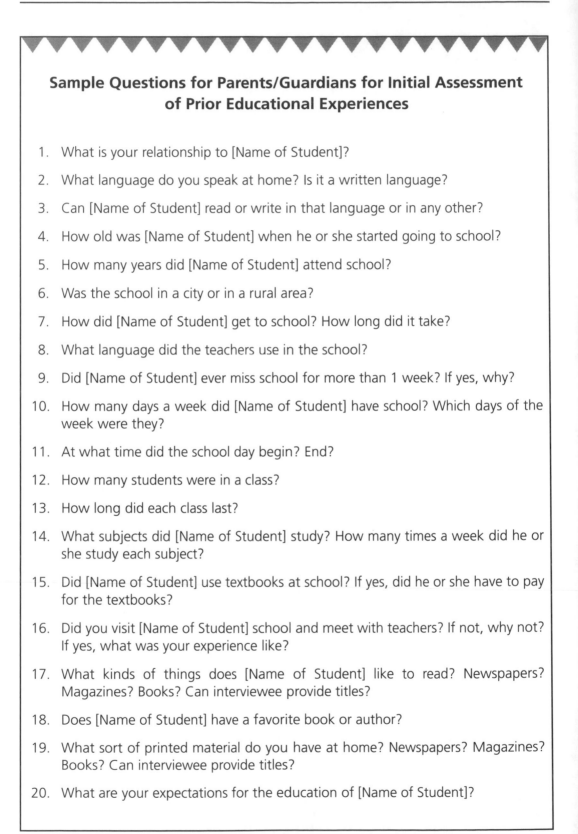

Sample Questions for Parents/Guardians for Initial Assessment of Prior Educational Experiences

1. What is your relationship to [Name of Student]?

2. What language do you speak at home? Is it a written language?

3. Can [Name of Student] read or write in that language or in any other?

4. How old was [Name of Student] when he or she started going to school?

5. How many years did [Name of Student] attend school?

6. Was the school in a city or in a rural area?

7. How did [Name of Student] get to school? How long did it take?

8. What language did the teachers use in the school?

9. Did [Name of Student] ever miss school for more than 1 week? If yes, why?

10. How many days a week did [Name of Student] have school? Which days of the week were they?

11. At what time did the school day begin? End?

12. How many students were in a class?

13. How long did each class last?

14. What subjects did [Name of Student] study? How many times a week did he or she study each subject?

15. Did [Name of Student] use textbooks at school? If yes, did he or she have to pay for the textbooks?

16. Did you visit [Name of Student] school and meet with teachers? If not, why not? If yes, what was your experience like?

17. What kinds of things does [Name of Student] like to read? Newspapers? Magazines? Books? Can interviewee provide titles?

18. Does [Name of Student] have a favorite book or author?

19. What sort of printed material do you have at home? Newspapers? Magazines? Books? Can interviewee provide titles?

20. What are your expectations for the education of [Name of Student]?

A COMFORTABLE INTERVIEW ATMOSPHERE

- Students should be interviewed about their past educational experiences in a relaxed, non-threatening environment. This can take place at the school, preferably in a class-room, library, or conference room, rather than in an office. It can also take place in the student's home, if feasible.
- For the interview to be productive, it is vital to establish a climate of trust, as well as a comfort zone. Students need to realize that everyone is there to help them.
- For those students and family members/guardians with no or low levels of English proficiency, the interview should be conducted in the native language with an inter-preter so that the interviewees may effectively communicate with school personnel.
- Educators will glean more information if they conduct the session so that it is a conversation or storytelling of the student/parent/guardian's past experiences rather than an intimidating machine-gun style of question and answer.

We suggest these topics on general family circumstances that we have observed as being effective in eliciting useful information about the ELL and in helping in the student's possible identification as SLIFE.

- What was the student's daily life like before coming to the United States?
- What were the student's living conditions like before immigrating?
- Was the student (or is the student) separated from family members? If so, from which members and for how long?
- Where/with whom did the student live before coming to the United States? For how long?
- Did the student live in refugee or resettlement centers prior to arrival in the United States? If so, where and for how long?
- Did the student live anywhere else in the United States? Where? For how long?

> We have to leave our home because of the war. We live in camp, my mother, my sisters, but we don't know nothing about my father and brothers and we have nothing and we wait to come here with my uncles.
>
> —Malik

> I come with my brother but my mother and other brothers stay home. I living with my father and sister and brother, but I miss my mother so much.
>
> —Estela

A sample interview sheet the school community can use when interviewing potential SLIFE appears on page 14. Discretion should be used in deciding which questions to include, and keep in mind that the interview session should avoid an intimidating question-answer style.

Sample Student Interview Questions Regarding Prior Schooling

Student's Name _____ Date of Evaluation _____

Interviewer _____

Interpreter's Name _____

Names/Relationship of Others Present _____

1. How many years did you go to school in your home country?

2. Did you go to school anywhere else? *If yes:* Where? How long?

3. How old where you when you started school?

4. Have you ever missed any school for more than 1 week? *If yes:* Tell me about it.

5. Was your school close to your home?

6. How did you get to school and how long did it take?

7. How many days a week did you go to school? Which days of the week?

8. What time did school start each day? What time did it end?

9. What language did your teachers speak in school?

10. What subjects did you study? Did you study them every day?

11. What are some of the things you did in class?

12. What kinds of school books did you have?

13. Tell me about a book that you like to read.

14. Did you learn the same kinds of things as you are learning here? Give me an example of something that is the same/different.

15. Tell me two things that are very different about school in the United States compared to school in your country.

16. With whom are you living in the United States?

Alternatives to Face-to-Face Interviews

Alternatives to face-to-face personal interviews exist, but these are likely to prove less effective. One alternative is to try to conduct the interview via telephone with the student's parent(s)/guardian(s). Key persons may have to be omitted from the dialogue, unless a telephone with conferencing capability is available at the school that would allow the parent coordinator(s), ESL instructor, translator, and other relevant school personnel to speak directly with the parent(s)/guardian(s).

Another alternative to personal interviews is to have the questionnaire translated into the language used at home and sent to the residence. The primary drawback to this method is that questionnaires are often not returned, whether because of literacy issues, lack of familiarity with such an instrument, or other reasons. There is also no way of guaranteeing that it is the student's parent/guardian who fills out the questionnaire rather than another person. A follow-up call to complete the questionnaire by phone may prove helpful. Again, interpretation services may be needed, so school personnel should see that adequate preparations have been made to have interpreters available or that the questionnaire has been accurately translated into the appropriate native language.

The chart that follows summarizes information-gathering options about the past schooling of SLIFE.

Although setting up interviews, arranging for interpreters, finding appropriate venues, and coordinating the schedules of several individuals is time-consuming and often frustrating, these efforts will pay off as they help to establish effective avenues of communication. Communication is the key to the SLIFE's past, because it will provide better understanding and will likely help open doors to the SLIFE's new future in the United States.

For interviews, the school community should keep these tips in mind.

TIPS FOR CONDUCTING EFFECTIVE INTERVIEWS

- Gaps in school attendance are often due to sensitive matters; therefore, it is essential that interviews be conducted in a sensitive and caring atmosphere.
- Informal "conversations" often elicit more information than formal, structured interviews.
- The interviews should be conducted in a quiet, relaxed environment without interruptions or where they can be kept to a minimum.
- Make sure the parents/guardians can communicate adequately in English. If not, a qualified interpreter must be present at the interview.
- Interpreters may be obtained through local educational agencies, community organizations, and religious organizations.

Because the needs of SLIFE are unique from those of most ELLs, responsible school personnel should take all the steps necessary to see that these students are properly identified. SLIFE are frequently placed in regular ESL and/or mainstream classes where they become lost, their frustrations mount, and all too often, they drop out. There have even been instances in which SLIFE, because of their limited literacy and academic skills, have been placed in special education classes, a too-common occurrence even with regular ELLs (Artiles, Trent, & Palmer, 2004; Brown, 2004).

Enrolling SLIFE in schools means that we must accept the requisite obligations to offer them the services and opportunities that enable them to feel that they belong in their new country and are motivated to become contributing citizens. The extra effort and time spent in the beginning to carefully screen these students will, in the long run, save time for all concerned. Above all, keep in mind that time is something high school SLIFE do not have enough of.

Profiles of Representative SLIFE

Five profiles representing some of the typical SLIFE who may be found in U.S. high schools follow.

Mamadou from Mali

At the age of 15, Mamadou immigrated to the United States from Mali. He had had no schooling in his home country and was not able to read or write when he enrolled in high school shortly after coming to the United States. Mamadou grew up in a rural area where there were few opportunities to interact with print, and his family could not afford to send him to the small village school. After arriving in the United States, Mamadou was placed in ninth grade because of his age. Two years later, Mamadou is able to speak fairly well, but his academic skills and reading and writing abilities are only at approximately a fourth-grade level.

> I never care about reading until I come here. In my country, nothing to read but here, everywhere print, words and signs and books and you have to read.
>
> —Mamadou

Sonia from the Dominican Republic

Sonia is from a rural area in the southern part of the Dominican Republic. She moves back and forth between the Dominican Republic and the United States. When Sonia is in the Dominican Republic, her school attendance is erratic. When she is in the United States, Sonia attends school more regularly, although at times she stays home from school to help out other family members. All in all, Sonia has missed several years of formal education, but exactly how many has been difficult to ascertain. She is in the eleventh grade, but her reading and writing proficiencies are at about a seventh grade level, and her spoken English is heavily accented, filled with colloquialisms, and very *Spanglish*.

> I no care about school home but here I like very much. The teachers they want help me, they teach me food, they very nice. I have many friend and I learn lots. Is hard for me sometimes because I must to stay home with my brothers when they sick or something. But I like school very much. Is good for me.
>
> —Sonia

Chang-Ching from China

Chang-Ching came to the United States a year ago at age 18. After leaving school in China at the end of eighth grade, he worked for a large international corporation in a big city until he was given permission to join his family in the United States. Again, because of Chang-Ching's age and despite his missed schooling, he was placed in the ninth grade. Chang-Ching's spoken English has become moderately fluent but retains a strong Cantonese accent. His writing is high-beginning level, but he has begun to show improvement. Chang-Ching strives to catch up with his classmates by working overtime. He spends most after-school hours at special programs for SLIFE such as reading and writing English and learning new skills in web design. Chang-Ching has found the school's bilingual program helpful. He believes that the bilingual teachers have a better understanding of the needs of SLIFE and that they teach so that students can understand both the language and the content.

> Hello! Everybody, my name is Chang-Ching. I'm 19 years old. I'm in HS study English. I like play computer game and play basketball. Eight month ago, I first time came a new country. I felt so afraid, because everything is stranger. But now, every thing I can do myself.
>
> —Chang-Ching

Brenda from Bosnia

At age 13, Brenda came with her family to the United States. Because she arrived during the spring semester, she only attended eighth grade for about two months. Brenda is now in her first year of high school. Her parents are college educated, but due to turmoil in the Balkans, Brenda's formal schooling was sporadic at best. Her mother tried to work with her at home but said that it was often impossible because there were too many "bad things happening," and the family was forced to make frequent moves. Brenda is happy to be here and happy to be in school but has many difficulties with even the basics. She reads at about a fifth-grade level; her oral proficiency is quite good, but her writing remains problematic.

> I love school. It's hard for me, but I work very hard all the time. I learn so much and I study all the time. Computers for me is the most wonderful. I want to go to college but I don't know what I want to study. Maybe doctor. Maybe computer person.
>
> —Brenda

Luis from Mexico

Luis is 15 years old and from a rural area of Mexico. His family—his father, mother, younger brother, and younger sister—are migrants who follow harvesting seasons. As a result, Luis frequently has gaps in attendance. His native language is Spanish, which he can read and write but only at a basic elementary level. He has just completed his first term of ninth grade at a U.S. school. His oral/aural abilities with English are good, as he often has to translate for his parents. Luis's written English and reading abilities indicate a third-grade level and his math is below grade level as well. He did not pass social studies or earth science.

The school does not have enough qualified ESL teachers to meet the needs of the sudden influx of Spanish-speaking students to the area, so SLIFE tend to be assigned to overpopulated classes with a broad range of ESL abilities. SLIFE attend mainstream classes in content areas, and some afternoon programs attempt to provide additional help via tutoring—but students often join their parents for landscaping work or in the fields and orchards for harvest after school and on weekends. As there will be no additional agricultural work until spring, the family will likely migrate elsewhere in search of work. Luis's teachers find him friendly and cooperative and think he would do well if he could remain in a given school for an extended period of time. However, given the economic circumstances of the family, this does not seem possible.

> I like school. Everyone care about me and I learn a lot and I have many friend and fun, but I have to help my family and when I go to the school no help and my parent, they need me and we go when there is work another place.
>
> —Luis

Although the five high school students profiled come from different countries and different backgrounds, they have several things in common:

- They have had less formal education than their ELL peers.
- They lack English-proficiency skills.
- They are not prepared for the grade-level work in the required subject areas.

Nevertheless, they are enthusiastic and motivated about their studies here, due in large part, as we will see later, to the dedication of their teachers.

Finally, it should be kept in mind that while SLIFE may lack academic knowledge and skills, they are quite likely to have witnessed or even been a part of life-changing events that have contributed to their acquiring a *knowledge of life*. These students enter schools with rich and varied experiences or "funds of knowledge"—that is, knowledge of mundane but necessary activities, whether animal husbandry, essential agricultural practices, artisan skills, or other "historically accumulated and culturally developed bodies of knowledge and skills essential for household or individual functioning and well-being" (Moll, Amanti, Neff, & Gonzalez, 1992, p. 133). SLIFE should not be considered deficient but rather as students who come with funds of knowledge that can and should be used as building blocks for the acquisition of new, academic knowledge.

Chapter 2

Literacy and Academic Language Proficiency

Literacy Skills

WHAT DOES IT MEAN TO BE LITERATE? *LITERATE* IS A TERM THAT IS USED OFTEN, USUALLY PRECEDED by a qualifier and resulting in expressions such as "computer literate," "media literate," or "information literate." Being literate within these domains means possessing different sets of skills that allow one to use a computer; navigate newspapers, television, and a variety of other media; or know where and how to find information. Most, however, agree that literacy skills are the tools one needs to read and write with fluency and comprehension. In the case of SLIFE, we need a more comprehensive definition of literacy skills because more is expected of them than just basic literacy. Meltzer's (2002) identification is inclusive and relevant for our purposes. She identifies literacy skill as a set of tools that learners use when they read, write, speak, listen, and think in order to learn; the same skills are also used to communicate or demonstrate that learning to others who need or would like to know.

A sound foundation in literacy skills is a basic prerequisite for academic success (August & Shanahan, 2006; Dalton, 1998). ELLs, in particular those newly enrolled in U.S. secondary schools, face the combined demands of acquiring literacy skills in English, as well as meeting content area knowledge standards, each with its own corpus of requisite, discipline-specific literacy skills more commonly referred to as *academic English*. Studies have shown that those ELLs with sound literacy skills in their native language usually make the transition to English more readily than those who lack basic literacy skills in their native language (Tartir, 2007), as is the case with SLIFE. These students thus face a greater challenge in making the transition to English literacy than other ELLs.

High school teachers are likely to encounter a range of literacy practices and skills among their SLIFE. These students may come from backgrounds in which printed materials have not been extensively available and, therefore, have had little to no significance in their daily lives. Some may have attended schools where printed materials and basic school supplies were very limited. They may not have been able to afford to buy newspapers, magazines, or books; they may come from families, cultures, or subcultures with low or no literacy and little reliance on print; or they may have come from heavily censored regimes that banned most printed materials.

Some students may be able to speak English but unable to read or write it. Some may be able to read and translate elementary texts but be unable to speak comprehensibly or understand English when it is spoken. Others may have little or no familiarity with the Roman alphabet or may be pre-literate in their native language. These are just some of the more salient variables that teachers of SLIFE may encounter in their classrooms at any given time. There are many more.

TYPES OF LITERACY OF SLIFE
• **Pre-literate:** Student has had no prior exposure to literacy skills; student's native language may not be written, newly written, and/or there may be few written materials available in their native language.
• **Non-literate:** Student's native language has a written form, but the student has not been exposed to literacy practices.
• **Semi-literate Roman alphabet:** Student has basic literacy skills but not enough to participate fully in grade-level schooling.
• **Non-alphabet literate:** Student has basic literacy skills in a different type of writing system. Student's literacy not strong in the native language and now the student must develop English literacy.

No matter which assessment instruments have been used to identify an ELL as SLIFE, teachers must still discern just what the literacy needs of their individual students are in order to build on what each SLIFE brings to class. Literacy development in English is affected by the literacy level of SLIFE in their native language, by their educational background, by their proficiency and literacy in English, and by their own goals and motivation. Faced with a wide variety of ability levels among the students in a high school SLIFE class, teachers in all disciplines are likely to find, at least initially, that it may be necessary to focus on elementary literacy skills using age-appropriate, cross-discipline texts and materials to determine the students' strengths and weaknesses. Many SLIFE need to learn that reading is a process through which readers construct meaning from text (Barr, Sadow, & Blachowicz, 1990; Slavin & Madden, 2001). Phonemic awareness, phonics, fluency, vocabulary, and text comprehension have been identified by the National Reading Panel (NICHD, 2000) as pivotal components of constructing meaning from text. Following are some suggestions that might help establish basic building blocks for academic success:

Alphabet Knowledge

These questions can be used as a guide to help teachers determine if SLIFE are familiar with the Roman alphabet.

- What is each student's native language?
- Does the native language (or any other language SLIFE may know) use the Roman alphabet or a different writing system, such as Cyrillic?
- Is the native language based on phonetics or is it ideogrammatic like Chinese?
- Do SLIFE know alphabet order?
- Can SLIFE alphabetize a simple word list?
- Do SLIFE know the difference between vowels and consonants?
- Can SLIFE spell their names correctly, using standard American English sounds for the Roman alphabet?
- Can SLIFE distinguish between cursive and print forms of the letters?

These are just a few of the questions that teachers should explore with SLIFE as early as possible in order to determine which building blocks of knowledge are already in place and which ones need to be added.

Phonology and Phonics

Because SLIFE have not yet developed strong, or even any, literacy skills, teachers should focus on developing students' *phonological awareness*—the ability to interpret letters as sounds and to recognize how combinations of letter strings become syllables and words. They also need to develop *phonemic awareness*; that is, it is necessary for SLIFE to become aware of individual speech sounds that combine to form words and phrases. Part of phonological awareness is learning to recognize how phrases, words, and syllables are represented in print (Gunning, 2008).

> When Nila came to the high school, the day after she arrived in the United States, she knew only a few words in English and had just about no literacy skills. We had to work with her on everything, and now she can read simple stories—easy passages—but she still has lots of problems with sound, letter, and word correspondence, rudimentary decoding skills, and basic words like *here, because, were*. She also has trouble forming letters. Writing is hard for her. When she copies words, they often look nothing like what they're supposed to and she confuses words and letters easily. But when you think about how little she came with and see what she's accomplished in the last five months, you can see how far she's come.
>
> —Gayle, HS Teacher of SLIFE

If native speakers of English are often confused by the variations of spelling and sounds, imagine how daunting the task of learning to spell in English can be with words like

-ough	schwa
slough	wa*fer*
rough	*fir*
through	*fur*
though	

Although English has many exceptions to spelling rules, there are several basic phonic patterns (orthography) that can and should be taught to SLIFE without going into details that would overwhelm them or interfere with focusing on important academic skills. Students should, for example, be able to distinguish between short vowels and long vowels in easily recognized patterns like

Short Vowels	Long Vowels
hat	hate
met	mete
bit	bite
tot	tote
jut	jute

More challenging orthography can be approached through the use of individual word lists kept by each SLIFE either as part of each student's vocabulary book (see Chapter 6) or in the form of lists posted on the classroom wall. The latter helps students realize they are not the only ones having trouble with certain words.

Morphemic variations should also be taught, in particular the addition of *–s* for plurals, *–'s* for the possessive, and *–(e)d* for the formation of regular past tense verbs. SLIFE will need to learn the change in meaning each of these morphemes imposes. Again, the purpose is to introduce and begin building literacy skills without introducing elements that overwhelm students. Textbooks for the various content areas can be used as sources for words to illustrate phonics lessons, thereby providing "vocabulary" within context.

One useful and fun exercise we encountered called "find the missing letter(s)" was used with SLIFE to reinforce phonics/orthography.

Use the letters *ch, v, z, f, g,* or *sh* to complete these words.

le__el   s__edule   chie__   al__ebra

__ampoo   __ampion   __ero   li__esa__er

Students enjoyed the challenge of this exercise and others like it. Sometimes, they came up with nonsense words, which made their classmates and themselves laugh. In general, they seem to like puzzles and derive a sense of accomplishment from working with them.

Print Materials

SLIFE with low or no literacy skills are oral rather than print-based learners. Print materials previously have had little significance in their daily lives. To help SLIFE become comfortable with print and develop their literacy skills, teachers should incorporate materials that have predictable linguistic elements, such as repetitive sentence patterns, rhyme, and alliteration, into learning. Predictable structures and patterns aid SLIFE in developing their understanding of text organization. Teachers should also make sure that there are numerous and varied visual elements in the text to provide nonlinguistic clues to meaning. Use graphics, graphic organizers, photos, pictures, and realia to help convey information. Illustrations or photos should be more than simply visually appealing and help SLIFE to understand meaning through culturally appropriate representations. Reading selections should be culturally relevant and motivate and engage students with situations and characters that are representative of their lives, experiences, and interests (Bennett, 2007).

For some SLIFE, even those who have literacy skills, it may be necessary to introduce them to the mechanics of high school subject textbooks. A basic activity is to take any textbook assigned to SLIFE and show them how to open an English textbook—that is, from right to left. (Remember that students who come from Arabic or Hebrew backgrounds may open their books from left to right—the reverse of English texts.) The teacher should query students about the information on the *title page*, and then explore the *table of contents* with them and its relationship to *body* or *contents* of the book. Careful attention should be paid to any *glossaries* that may be found in the text, as this is a good source for vocabulary words. The *index* is another section of the text the teacher can explore with SLIFE in order to help them find relevant information more easily and efficiently.

After introducing the parts of a textbook, the teacher may want to explore the types of printed materials that were available in each student's native country. Were there newspapers and magazines? Were there many periodicals? What kinds? Were they expensive? What books have the students read in the past? What are their favorites? To further increase awareness of printed matter in the United States and find out more about the personal interests of SLIFE, teachers may ask students to bring a magazine in any language to class for discussion about contents and why they chose that particular publication.

Generally, SLIFE need to work on narrative skills. Initially, teachers will need to focus on chronological sequence and character(s). It is very important that teachers of SLIFE emphasize chronological sequence, as this is a basic writing/reporting skill that students will have to use repeatedly across content areas throughout their high school experience. Students can start by sharing their stories aloud—even in their native language or using a combination of their native language and English if necessary—and then make the transition to writing the story as part of the individual portfolio (see Chapter 7).

Autobiographical books (see Chapter 6) are a good technique once students have developed letter formation and other basic literacy skills. Literature Circles, Reading Buddies, and Think-Pair-Share, which are used extensively in regular English Language Arts classes and in ESL, are particularly valuable in promoting SLIFE literacy. In Think-Pair-Share (Kagan, 1989), students first listen to the teacher's question and then have time to think about their responses. Next, they pair up with classmates and discuss their responses; and finally, each pair shares its response with the rest of the class. Because this activity combines oral literacy and collaboration, it closely follows the generally preferred learning modes of most SLIFE (see Chapter 3).

Teachers can use some of the same essential strategies that are important in the development of literacy skills for all ELLs, particularly for SLIFE.

- Provide a print-rich environment: Because many SLIFE come from homes and environments where print is not part of their daily lives, teachers should surround them with print. Whenever possible, create word walls, and hang student writing and other print materials throughout the classroom. Establish a reading corner with basic readers for students to check out.

> My home, we no have book, no newspaper, nobody read but me now and my sister because of school. Not like here school. Everybody here have book, notebook, we can take book home, not just textbook but my teacher have little book I like read and now my sister look book too.
>
> —Habiba, SLIFE

- Supplement print with extensive use of visuals. Print can be overwhelming for SLIFE.

Because reading and writing are so integral to the daily lives of educators, they often find it difficult to grasp just how overwhelming print can be for SLIFE. To have a sense of how SLIFE feel, imagine being asked to read this piece of writing or something like it:

Nothing about it is familiar, and you are probably even unsure in which direction to read; is it read from left to right, from right to left, from top to bottom, or from bottom to top? This uncertainty is analogous to how SLIFE often feel when confronted with the print demands of secondary school texts.

To help SLIFE become familiar and comfortable with print and develop their literacy skills, teachers should encourage many types of reading: whole-class reading, shared reading, buddy reading, and independent reading. Have easy readers or picture books available for SLIFE to check out on their own. Give them a sense of ownership in the process of reading development.

Picture Books

For SLIFE with basic literacy skills, carefully selected picture books can provide valuable content material support. When selecting picture books, SLIFE teachers should make sure these texts are of high interest to secondary students, do not include too many idiomatic structures, and convey information relevant to the mainstream curriculum. Some picture books popular in SLIFE classes we have visited are listed in Table 1. This list is a sample of picture books that can be used at the secondary level to develop English proficiency, literacy skills, and academic content knowledge. The language is accessible, the illustrations are attractive and informative without being childish, and the material is interesting and instructional.

Academic Language Proficiency

In addition to developing their literacy skills, SLIFE, like all ELLs, must develop academic language proficiency. Because students' achievement is closely correlated with academic language proficiency (Ehevarria, Vogt, & Short, 2008), without it, they will have little chance of academic success. Academic language proficiency differs significantly from everyday conversational language (Cummins, 1981, 1984, 2000). Crucial aspects of academic language include understanding and being able to use the vocabulary of each discipline, and engaging in higher-level thinking skills such as explanation, analysis, argumentation, and persuasion (Gunning, 2003; Short, 2002b). To develop the academic language proficiency necessary for success in school, SLIFE need frequent opportunities to engage in structured classroom interactions related to academically relevant content.

Vocabulary

As content demands become greater, so does the complexity of language, making the situation even more difficult for SLIFE struggling with the basics. One area with increasingly demanding content is vocabulary. The amount of vocabulary needed to understand the language of specific disciplines presents a major obstacle for all ELLs

TABLE 1: Popular Picture Books for SLIFE

African American

Author	Most Recent Edition	Title
Ringgold, F.	2003	*If a Bus Could Talk: The Story of Rosa Parks*
Siegelson, K.	1999	*In the Time of Drums*
William, S. A.	1997	*Working Cotton*

Alphabet, Spelling, and Vocabulary

Author	Most Recent Edition	Title
Ringgold, F.	2004	*Cassie's Word Quilt*
Viorst, J.	1997	*The Alphabet from Z to A*

Americas

Author	Most Recent Edition	Title
Yolen, J.	1996	*Encounter*

Environmental Studies / Science

Author	Most Recent Edition	Title
Cherry, L.	2000	*The Great Kapok Tree*
Kalman, B., & Dyer, H.	2006	*Savanna Food Chains*
Van Allsburg, C.	1992	*Just a Dream*
Willis, N.	2006	*Red Knot: A Shorebird's Incredible Journey*

Immigration (European)

Author	Most Recent Edition	Title
Bartone, E.	1997	*Peppe the Lamplighter*
Cech, J.	1998	*My Grandmother's Journey*
Tarbescu, E.	1998	*Annushka's Voyage*

Math

Author	Most Recent Edition	Title
Adler, D.	2009	*Working with Fractions*
Demi	1997	*One Grain of Rice*
Pinczes, E.	2003	*Inchworm and a Half*
Pinczes, E.	2002	*A Remainder of One*
Pinczes, E.	1999	*One Hundred Hungry Ants*
Scieszka, J., & Smith, L.	1995	*Math Curse*

TABLE 1 (continued)

Multicultural

Author	Most Recent Edition	Title
Levy, J. Trans: M. Arisa	2006	*Celebrate! It's Cinco de Mayo*
Messinger, C., & Katz, S.	2007	*When the Shadbush Blooms*
Sisulu, E.	1999	*The Day Gogo Went to Vote*
Stanley, S.	1998	*Monkey Sunday: A Story from a Congolese Village*
Yin	2006	*Brothers*

U. S. History

Author	Most Recent Edition	Title
Adler, D., & Himler, R.	2003	*A Picture Book of Lewis and Clark*
Adler, D., & Himler, R.	2007	*A Picture Book of John Hancock*
Stemple, H.E., Yolen, J., & Roth, R.	2003	*Roanoke: The Lost Colony—An Unsolved Mystery from History*

Vietnam War

Author	Most Recent Edition	Title
Bunting, E.	1990	*The Wall*
Bunting, E., & Diaz, D.	1998	*Going Home*

World War II Era

Author	Most Recent Edition	Title
Smith, F.D.	2008	*My Secret Camera: Life in the Lodz Ghetto*
Welch, C.	2000	*Children of the Relocation Camps*

(Moje, Collazo, Carillos, & Marx, 2001; Watts-Taffe & Truscott, 2000), especially for SLIFE. Norms of discourse vary across disciplines (Hyland, 2004), and even words that may be familiar to SLIFE take on new and very different discipline-specific meanings. To succeed in science students need to understand the language of science. In a mainstream earth science class, for instance, the word *buckle* came up. We observed SLIFE whispering to one another, trying to make sense of this use of the word. Apparently, they had learned this word previously as that "thing on you belt," but they had no idea how it might relate to the current science lesson in the context of a discussion about how the "earth buckles in certain places."

Teaching vocabulary has traditionally been a heavily emphasized element of any ESL instruction. But how does the ESL teacher go about quickly and efficiently building up the vocabularies of SLIFE? Although content-based instruction has been widely accepted as the best way to effectively promote academic language proficiency while simultaneously developing content knowledge (Brinton, Snow, & Wesche, 2003; Echevarria et al., 2008), important questions remain as to how to best go about such instruction for SLIFE at the secondary level (DeCapua et al., 2007). SLIFE often lack a basic vocabulary; this inhibits their ability to speak comprehensibly, to read with understanding, and to write. In order to help SLIFE develop the vocabulary they need to negotiate their new environment, teachers may want to explore, at least initially, some of the following suggestions.

Sight Words

Sight words are words that appear with high frequency in reading as well as in spoken everyday English and written English. Being familiar with these words without having to struggle with decoding them facilitates faster reading (May, 1998). As to which words fall into this category, researchers have determined that some 100 of these sight words constitute approximately fifty percent of what we read (Fry, Kress, & Foun-toukidis, 2004). These include some of the most common words in English. Fry et al. (2004) provides a list of 300 instant sight words that serve as a good starting point with SLIFE. Teachers can create word lists and display them around the classroom or print out and distribute them to each student. These words should be brought to the attention of students often, until they assimilate them into their vocabularies. The first 100 on the list are shown in Table 2.

TABLE 2: Sight Words

a	can	her	many	see	us
about	come	here	me	she	very
after	day	him	much	so	was
again	did	his	my	some	we
all	do	how	new	take	were
an	down	I	no	that	what
and	eat	if	not	the	when
any	for	in	of	their	which
are	from	is	old	them	who
as	get	it	on	then	will
at	give	just	one	there	with
be	go	know	or	they	work
been	good	like	other	this	would
before	had	little	our	three	you
boy	has	long	out	to	your
but	have	make	put	two	
by	he	man	said	up	

Resource Tip

All 300 of Fry's list of most common sight words are available at http://literacyconnections.com/Dolch.php.

Affixes

In "Resources About English Language Literacy, Academic Language, and Content Area Literacy," Tartir (2007) emphasizes the importance of learning vocabulary through the study of roots and affixes, a powerful tool in helping students uncover the meanings of new words. Knowing twenty common prefixes and fourteen roots, for example, can open the door to the meaning of over 100,000 words (Gruber, 1986).

Resource Tip

Building Vocabulary: Prefixes, Roots, and Suffixes, by J. Wilde, lists some of the most productive affixes and roots in English and is available at www.ncela.gwu.edu/resabout/literacy/Building_Vocabulary.pdf.

In order to enhance SLIFE vocabulary development across content areas, ESL teachers should work closely with their colleagues in other disciplines. For example, focusing ESL lessons on the prefix *geo–* will help students with terms such as *geology* in the earth sciences, *geometry* in mathematics, and *geography* in social studies. Teachers can reinforce lessons with exercises that provide immediate feedback and assessment, as in the following example.

Add the prefix *geo–* or the prefix *bio–* to each word below to match its meaning:

_____ *graphy*: the story of a person's life
_____ *logy*: science that studies earth's physical structure and history
_____ *logy*: study of living organisms
_____ *graphy*: the study of the earth, its atmosphere, and human activity

---

Once students demonstrate that they have learned the words, they can be asked to use the words in original sentences and include them in their vocabulary books (see Chapter 6).

As discussed extensively by Echevarria et al. (2008), the study of language through content allows SLIFE to develop language skills while building subject-area knowledge and supports the simultaneous development of the different skill areas (speaking, listening, reading, writing). The language acquisition of SLIFE is boosted by the meaningful use of language through material that is relevant and essential to their schooling. SLIFE teachers must therefore work closely with mainstream content teachers to develop appropriate standards-based lessons that include both language and content-area objectives.

> What works for me in class is the reading. It help me learn know the pronunciation and how to read the words that are heard for me to read or to pronouns. I like everything that we do in class because I learn more and more. I like all the other class except social studies because some time I don't know how to read the words or describe some thing it was heard before or by writing I do so many mistake and she doesn't understanding what I read or what I mean to say.
>
> —Katia

For teachers of SLIFE, literacy has to be considered, at least initially, in its most basic sense—in terms of the skills students need in order to read and write in English. Developing oral/aural skills and transferring these to print and written production are the first steps along the way to the acquisition of academic skills. Needless to say, patience at this stage is an absolute prerequisite of all concerned, as repetition, correction, and reinforcement are necessary in order to establish the building blocks on which later, more advanced skills will depend. There are resources available to ESL teachers, most immediately input from a recognized reading expert either in the school, the district, or consulting from outside. Keep in mind that most SLIFE need an *introduction* to phonics, phonemics, and orthography—not an in-depth study of these areas. Once they have a sound grounding in the basics of word attack and decoding, they will be able to sort out these linguistic elements of English and need less help with them. At this point, teacher and student can begin emphasizing academic English and higher-level cognitive skills development.

Resource Tip

Helpful Literacy Websites

www.cal.org/topics/le/
www.ncela.gwu.edu/resabout/literacy/
http://literacyconnections.com/
http://crede.berkeley.edu/standards/standards.html

Chapter 3

Educating the Whole Child

DURING THE PAST SEVERAL DECADES, WE HAVE SEEN WESTERN MEDICINE ADAPT PRACTICES FROM Eastern medicine to offer a more holistic approach to treating patients. Rather than simply diagnose and treat a patient's physical symptoms, doctors consider the whole person, exploring emotional and social factors in the patient's life as well. We strongly advocate a parallel holistic approach in dealing with the education of SLIFE.

As shown in previous chapters, SLIFE have various needs that differ from other ELLs, often rendering traditional ESL or bilingual programs inadequate (Mace-Matluck et al., 1998; Ruiz-de-Velasco & Fix, 2000; Walsh, 1999). SLIFE require special programs that address their specific needs, not all of which are academic. However, because language and academic issues are so critical for high school SLIFE, educators tend to focus their attention and resources on addressing these areas, downplaying or even neglecting the many affective needs of SLIFE. It has been our experience that in order to effectively educate the whole child, affective issues must be considered in the planning and execution of a successful program for SLIFE.

ELLs, by virtue of having left their home cultures and languages, have social and affective needs related to language learning and cultural adjustment. As ELLs learn English, they ordinarily develop a second "identity" or a new "language ego," that is, different ways of behaving and thinking (Brown, 2007). In the process, ELLs often face affective issues concerning self and identify (Norton, 2000), and SLIFE even more so. The combination of the U.S. secondary school experience with the demands of learning English frequently has an even greater impact on the emotional lives of SLIFE, often creating within them a sense of insecurity, inadequacy, and helplessness.

In the 1940s, Abraham Maslow, an early leader in humanistic psychology, proposed a hierarchy of needs or drives affecting human behavior. Maslow ranked these needs in order of decreasing priority, or potency, but increasing sophistication: physiological needs, safety, belongingness and love, esteem, need to know and understand, aesthetic needs, self-actualization, and transcendence (see Figure 2). Only when the more primitive needs are met can an individual progress to higher levels in the hierarchy (Maslow, 1943). SLIFE suffering from post-traumatic stress disorder (PTSD), or the stresses of experiences such as separation from family, culture shock, and/or school shock will be more focused on the lower levels of the self. Because meeting their basic needs will, at least to some degree, monopolize their attention until these are met, SLIFE may have difficulty learning and making academic gains. Likewise, those SLIFE for whom economic issues are daily concerns and who must work to supplement family income are more concerned with the lower levels of the hierarchy than the higher levels as represented by the pursuit of education.

FIGURE 2:   Maslow's Hierarchy of Needs

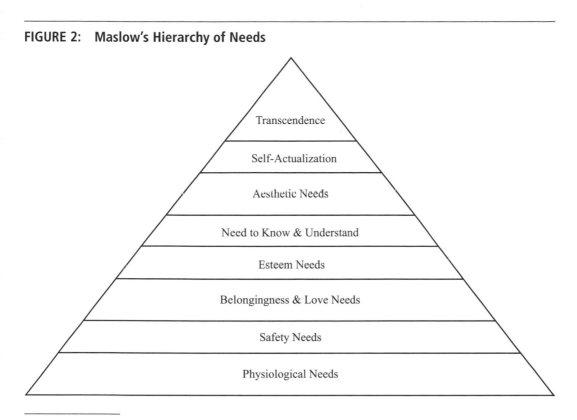

Transcendence

Self-Actualization

Aesthetic Needs

Need to Know & Understand

Esteem Needs

Belongingness & Love Needs

Safety Needs

Physiological Needs

Source: Adapted and used with permission of Pearson Education.

Psychological Issues

Many SLIFE face psychological problems as a result of having been transplanted from the familiar people, language, and surroundings in their home country to a new environment and a new language. Some SLIFE have been profoundly and adversely affected by civil war and other types of violence or upheaval in their home country from which they fled and where they may have lost family members and friends. Some of these issues may be potentially explosive and should be approached with sensitivity, care, and understanding. It is often necessary to address emotional needs before the academic ones.

Post-Traumatic Stress Disorder

SLIFE coming from areas of communal violence, war-torn regions, or areas that have suffered severe natural disasters, may suffer from post-traumatic stress disorder (PTSD). The severity of symptoms depends on various factors, including SLIFE's perceptions of safety and protection in the new environment. Symptoms of PTSD usually develop when an individual realizes that he or she is in a safe environment and can reflect on the traumatic events experienced (Arroyo & Eth, 1996). Symptoms of PTSD may not be initially evident and may differ widely, but the most common include withdrawal from group activities; agitation; sleep disturbances; physical symptoms such as headaches or stomach problems; depression and self-destructive behaviors; and/or unexplained outbursts of anger, among others.

Resource Tip

Two websites from www.kidshealth.org provide a good basic overview of PTSD:

www.kidshealth.org/teen/your_mind/mental_health/ptsd.html
www.kidshealth.org/parent/positive/talk/ptsd.html

Recognizing PTSD in SLIFE is important, because learning can be seriously affected in students suffering from this disorder. Depending on the nature and extent of the student's symptom(s) and his or her level of English proficiency, it may be possible for the teacher and/or the school counselor to establish an initial avenue of communication. Referral to a psychologist or psychiatrist may be necessary, particularly in the cases of more extreme symptoms and behaviors. Ideally, the professional should be bilingual; although realistically, this may not always be possible. At the very least, SLIFE should be referred to a professional with extensive experience in working with culturally different populations.

Despite the best efforts of school personnel to encourage and facilitate professional help, such efforts may be rejected if outside counseling is negatively perceived by members of a given culture. In such instances, it may help school personnel to enlist the help of someone the family and student trust, for example, a religious leader or community representative.

Culture Shock

> When I first come here, I love everything. Everything so wonderful, my uncle, he take us to Statue of Liberty. and to see skyscraper. But then I miss my mother, I miss my friend, I miss my sister, I miss everything, I'm so sad. Now I still miss my mother, my family back home, but I'm happy too because I can go the school and learning so much and having other friends.
>
> —Jorge

Culture shock is the feeling people experience when they spend any length of time in another culture and begin to realize that their understanding and interpretation of the world and the behaviors around them differ from, and often conflict with, those of the new culture (DeCapua & Wintergerst, 2004). Anyone entering a new culture for an extended period of time is subject to culture shock and faces different stages of adjustment, often referred to as the U-Curve of Adjustment (Lysgaard, 1955) (see page 35). Oberg (1966) suggests that there are four stages of culture shock.

FIGURE 3: The U-Curve of Cultural Adjustment

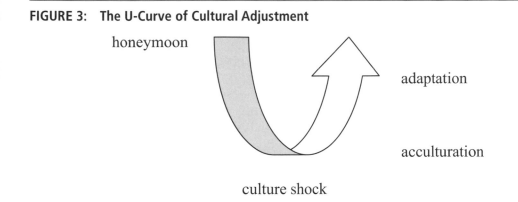

honeymoon

adaptation

acculturation

culture shock

The first stage is called the **honeymoon phase** because newly arrived immigrants find everything wonderful and exciting. After a time, however, the euphoria and elation fade, and immigrants enter the second phase, **culture shock**. In this stage, people feel overwhelmed by everything and begin to feel frustrated, unhappy, disappointed, and depressed. Often they become angry toward the new country, its culture, and its people. What was formerly exciting and interesting now becomes irritating and annoying; how things are done "back home" seems the "right" way, while the ways in the new country seem wrong, inappropriate, or inferior. For teenagers, who are already suffering from the typical teen identity issues, adjustment to a new culture with different expectations and roles related to gender, age, and social behavior can be particularly difficult. The resulting emotional distress can cause physical symptoms such as sleeplessness, weight gain or loss, and/or digestive problems. Psychological signs include withdrawal, depression, and/or extreme fatigue.

As immigrants become more comfortable with the new culture, their surroundings, and the language, they enter the third stage of adjustment, **acculturation**. At this stage, immigrants begin to adapt to the new culture. They soon realize that there are aspects they like and don't like both in the new culture and in their own culture. With such awareness, they are able to begin finding their own way in the new culture. Finally, when they more fully adjust to the new culture, they move into the final phase, the recovery or **adaptation** stage. At this point, immigrants are reconciled to and more understanding of the new culture, accepting of both the good and the bad and generally ready to adapt to life in the new country.

If teachers find SLIFE exhibiting any or a combination of these traits, it is important that they try to talk with them and, if appropriate, refer them to counseling/guidance services:

- depression
- extreme tiredness or fatigue
- illnesses not attributable to viral or bacterial infections (e.g., severe acid indigestion, headaches)
- unusual anger and/or frustration
- significant increase in appetite and consequent weight gain

School Shock

In addition to culture shock, SLIFE also face school shock. For those who had some formal education in their home country, U.S. schools may present a very different set of experiences. For those who have never formally attended school, or who have had significant gaps in their education, the basics of classroom behavior may prove challenging, simply because these students do not fully understand what is expected of them. These SLIFE need to learn basic school behaviors such as sitting at a desk, holding and using a writing implement, and/or requesting a hall pass—routine behaviors that are frequently confusing, awkward, and overwhelming for them.

Take a few moments and think about the different classroom behaviors you expect of your students, in addition to the ones already listed.

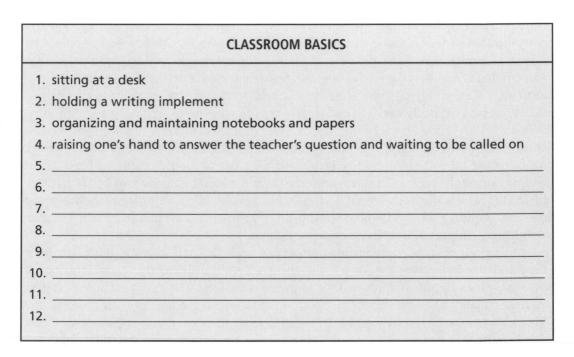

CLASSROOM BASICS

1. sitting at a desk
2. holding a writing implement
3. organizing and maintaining notebooks and papers
4. raising one's hand to answer the teacher's question and waiting to be called on
5. _____
6. _____
7. _____
8. _____
9. _____
10. _____
11. _____
12. _____

Completing such a list helps secondary school teachers explicitly identify some behaviors that they may expect their students to know already, because these are behaviors that are generally learned by students as part of the early schooling process, well before they reach the high school level. Even within a given class period, SLIFE may need help understanding the different behaviors expected from them, such as the move from a teacher's modeling of a learning activity, to group work, to individual tasks. Careful guidance from the teacher, with the help of other more experienced SLIFE (see the Easing the Transition section, page 38) should help the newer SLIFE adjust to new behavioral expectations and diminish their feelings of school shock.

In addition to lacking familiarity with classroom behaviors, some newly arrived SLIFE may be unfamiliar with basic school facilities such as student cafeterias, gyms, locker rooms, computer labs, or even indoor plumbing, and will need explanations of how to find these facilities and how they function. School routines and practices are also likely to be different and/or unfamiliar than those SLIFE have previously experienced. For example, students are expected to follow very specific steps in a cafeteria, such as forming lines or clearing their trays in a certain way. Some staircases are "up" staircases while others are "down." State laws also require parents/guardians to sign permission forms for a range of activities, from allowing students' photos to be published in the school newspaper to permitting students to go on field trips and everything else in between. The notion of a "permission slip" may be unknown to SLIFE parents/guardians and can be especially problematic if they themselves are pre-literate.

To form a clearer picture of the types of school routines and practices SLIFE and/or their parents/guardians need to understand in your school, complete this chart. Some examples have been given to help you in your thinking.

IN SCHOOL	AFTER SCHOOL
1. Cafeteria etiquette and behaviors (including line formation and clean-up)	9. Clubs (purpose, how to join, why to join them)
2. _____	10. _____
3. _____	11. _____
4. _____	12. Permission slips (why required, for what, who can sign)
5. State-mandated vaccinations and health screenings (different types; why, how, and where to get them)	13. _____
	14. _____
6. _____	15. _____
7. _____	
8. School passes (different types, when they are used, where to get them)	16. Parent-teacher conferences (their purpose, times held)

Making such lists and keeping them handy can serve a number of purposes. They can be used as suggestions for some of the topics to be covered in initial conferences with parents/guardians of SLIFE and during their tours of the school. Some of these topics can serve as starting points for group discussion and may involve more than one teacher; for example, a discussion of the need for physical education and the use of the gym or issues of good hygiene could be presented in conjunction with the gym and/or biology teachers or the school nurse. On a simpler basis, referring to the lists after several months of school can permit the teacher to see just how far the SLIFE have come since the first day.

Easing the Transition

> When I came here, I know nothing, I very scare but my
> teacher, she tell Alberto, you work with him, you his friend,
> and Alberto, he help me with everything and I feel good.
>   —Andrés

Providing a peer mentor or "buddy" can greatly ease a SLIFE's transition to the new school environment. SLIFE who have been in the United States for a longer period of time are designated to serve as "buddies" for more recently arrived SLIFE. The more experienced students help the new ones as much as possible with explanations of basic classroom activities such as teachers' instructions, daily routines, and school requirements. As someone who understands what the newcomer is going through, a buddy provides the newcomer with a feeling of safety and security. In addition, the pairing of newly arrived SLIFE with those who have been in the United States longer allows the latter to reinforce and practice what they have learned (Fu, 2003) and to develop their own self-confidence.

A BUDDY
• eases the transition for newly arrived SLIFE
• empathizes and understands the needs of newly arrived SLIFE
• provides an anchor for the new student in what may be a radically new and/or different school environment

Humanistic Approaches to Working with SLIFE

In order to develop successful programs, it is important to understand that SLIFE are generally members of high-context (Hall, 1976), collectivistic cultures (Triandis, 1995) that view the world through "pre-scientific spectacles" (Flynn, 2007). Understanding the attitudes, perceptions, and expectations of individuals from high-context, collectivistic cultures will provide educators with insights into the learning paradigm of SLIFE and allow teachers and others to better understand how these students learn best (DeCapua & Marshall, forthcoming). An important aspect of high-context, collectivistic cultures (or sub-cultures) is the strong sense members have of belonging to one's group. In such cultures, one's group—a large shared network with a mutual sense of shared obligations, responsibilities, and belonging—is primary (DeCapua & Wintergerst, 2004; Hofstede, 2005; Triandis, 1995). People from high-context, collectivistic cultures, especially oral and rural ones, do not easily or often interact with strangers or relative strangers. Members of these cultures fulfill important roles for other people who are part of their network, that is, those with whom they have some sort of a relationship. From such a conception of *relationship*, teachers, by virtue of their role in students' lives, become part of students' relationships or networks. Once this relationship is established, it must be maintained by ongoing two-way communication between the teacher and the student, the teacher and the family, and the entire school community and the family (Marshall, 1998). It is important to build on these relationships in order to encourage parent/guardian involvement with the school (see Chapter 7).

People with a pre-scientific or pragmatic, as opposed to a scientific, or academic worldview typically do not engage in the types of cognitive thinking (e.g., formal problem solving and abstract reasoning) traditionally associated with formal Western-style schooling (Flynn, 2007; Rogoff & Chavajay, 1995; Tulviste, 1991). SLIFE, who have not fully participated in formal Western-style schooling, may not yet have developed cognitive skills characterized by solving problems on a formal level nor are they likely to have engaged in abstract reasoning removed from the concrete world and real experiences (Flynn, 2007; Akinnaso, 1992; Mehan, 1979). Their learning experiences are instead likely to have been characterized by immediate, concrete relevancy and the practical skills of daily life. Effective programs for SLIFE are those that understand and take into account the affective, cognitive, and cultural learning needs of this population.

Educational approaches, best practices, and activities must find a middle ground between the needs of SLIFE and the expectations of the U.S. school system in order to facilitate SLIFE learning, to help SLIFE make a successful transition to formal schooling, and to support the development of these students' higher-level cognitive skills. DeCapua & Marshall (forthcoming) and Marshall (1998) suggest a "Mutually Adaptive Learning Paradigm (MALP)" to facilitate the transition of SLIFE to U.S. schooling. Briefly, the paradigm consists of three essential steps: (1) Accept the conditions SLIFE need in order to learn, including a strong relationship with teachers; (2) Design lessons that combine processes from their learning paradigm with that of the United States, with a strong emphasis on collaborative learning and scaffolding and a combination of oral and written learning modes; and (3) Focus on activities that use familiar language and content while developing the cognitive skills or academic worldview of SLIFE. (See DeCapua & Marshall, forthcoming, and Marshall, 1998, for further discussion.)

For SLIFE, a supportive learning environment is particularly important and conducive to successful learning outcomes. Along with incorporating MALP, teachers should engage in facilitative teaching (Rogers, 1966; Rogers & Freiberg, 1994). In this approach, the teacher is a facilitator rather than an authority, and learning takes into account both affective and cognitive development. Teachers who are facilitators are responsive to students' feelings and emotional needs, dialogue with students and avoid lecturing, praise and give positive feedback, tailor material to students' needs, and are aware of cultural and cognitive backgrounds (DeCapua, 2008a; Rogers & Freiberg, 1994). Liu & Tang (2008) offer these five best practices based on a humanistic approach to teaching that have proven effective in tending to the affective needs of SLIFE:

1. Create a caring learning community in which the basic needs of SLIFE are met.
2. Create a learning climate that leads to relaxed alertness—that is, an environment in which SLIFE are challenged but not stressed.
3. Create a meaningful learning environment.
4. Use multiple ways to teach SLIFE.
5. Encourage both independent and collaborative learning.

Alternative Goals

For some older SLIFE who enter high school with very limited literacy and academic skills and insufficient time to compensate for lost education, it may be necessary to develop alternative programs and goals. In these cases, teachers and administrators must focus on skills that will most benefit the students rather than those necessary for test performance, meeting state standards, and/or maintaining the school's assessment ratings. For the benefit of the student, teachers must focus on the development of students' basic literacy skills, proficiency in reading and writing English, knowledge of general mathematics, and basic understanding of the United States and state governments, necessary for full participation as a citizen. The question the school community must ask is: What can we, as educators, do to help SLIFE find jobs and take their places in society?

An effective SLIFE program takes into consideration the whole child, as shown.

ACADEMIC/INSTRUCTIONAL NEEDS	AFFECTIVE NEEDS
• literacy skills development • basic English language proficiency • the development of academic English proficiency • English proficiency to meet state English Language Arts standards • subject-area support, both knowledge and skills • preparation for high-stakes assessments • cognitive development of an academic worldview	• introduction to the norms of the U.S. classroom and to school culture • social, emotional, and psychological support, especially if students have faced family separation, war, or other traumatic experiences • social-identity formation, issues of self-esteem, and developing a sense of place and belonging • development of social support network and positive relationships with peers, teachers, and school support staff • culture shock support • cultural adaptation and acceptance

Case Study: Leon, A 16-Year-Old 10th Grader from Sierra Leone

Leon emigrated two years ago from Sierra Leone in West Africa to the United States. Leon lives with his mother who works as a hospital aide. He has a brother and a sister who also live in the United States. Leon speaks Creole with his mother and English with his siblings. Leon did not previously attend school in his home country because of a civil war there.

When Leon first came to the United States, he was placed in ninth grade because of his age and despite the fact that he had had no prior schooling whatsoever. While he has learned to speak English quite fluently, his reading level is significantly below grade level. Leon is in an intermediate ESL/SLIFE program and barely passing. His grades for the first three marking periods of the current school year were as follows: ESL—65, 50, and 65; English Language Arts—65, 60, and 60; Science—65, 65, and 70; Math 70, 75, and 75.

When asked by one of the authors as to why his grades in math and science were better than in ESL and English, Leon said, "Science is my favorite subject, and I always curious about the nature." He added with a smile, "I like the math teacher." My math teacher make math fun. He plays math games, play with numbers, and teach us how to solve word problems. He help me too. I feel comfortable and learn a lot in his class." Leon also talked about his poor grades in ESL. According to Leon, the ESL teacher was too busy taking care of the many newly immigrated students to give him any attention. "Almost every week we have new kid coming with zero English," Leon commented.

Leon loves the after-school program for SLIFE students. He noted, "This program makes me stay at school longer and makes me learn. I also like to stay with my friends and learn together. I used to go to the park with my skateboard, and you know," he added, "it's likely to get into trouble there, you know." He also enjoys using the school computer to do his projects and search the Internet: "I have no computer at home. I don't have a lot of things my friends have at home." On days where there is no after-school program, Leon hangs out with friends.

Commentary on the Case Study

Why does Leon do relatively well in his math and science classes? First, as far as science is concerned, he likes the subject because it supports his natural curiosity about nature. Students learn best what they want and need to know (Gage & Berliner, 1991). In Leon's case, his interest in science has motivated him to study hard. And the more he learns, the more easily and quickly he takes in new information.

Second, in the case of math, he likes the teacher because the teacher makes learning meaningful and attends to students' affective needs. The teacher facilitates learning rather than simply lecturing, encouraging rather than criticizing and responding to their feelings. The teacher also addresses the learning needs of individual students such as Leon, rather than teaching to the tests.

Leon also mentioned how much he loved the after-school program for SLIFE. Thinking back to Maslow's hierarchy presented earlier in this chapter, we see how Leon's affective needs relate to his learning. The program allows him to work with other SLIFE; to do homework in an environment conducive to learning; to get individual, focused attention from teachers; and to have access to computers and other learning resources. In other words, his basic needs of safety and belongingness are satisfied through the after-school program, and his attention is thus turned to learning—a higher need on Maslow's hierarchy.

Chapter 4

Program Models

> I'm the stars, I'm the night.
> When we are together, we are the sun.
> We fight for who we are.
> What would we be if we don't fight back?
> We are power.
> Our life is not a barren field, we will not be frozen with snow.
> Our life is not a broken-winged bird, that cannot fly.
>
> —Nelson

GIVEN THE DIVERSITY OF THE SLIFE POPULATION, THERE IS NO ONE PROGRAM THAT CAN SERVE AS a single model that will meet all the needs of the different learners. Basically, there are six models of SLIFE programs that, on the whole, are very similar to programs for ELLs. The key difference is that SLIFE require even more than ELLs of everything these programs provide: more time, more individual attention, more scaffolding, more differentiation, and more support in all areas.

Newcomer Program Model

Districts that have large numbers of ELLs and/or SLIFE may, when feasible, elect to establish high schools uniquely focused on the needs of this student population. These schools are variously known as Newcomer High Schools, International High Schools, or Academies.

Newcomer programs are created specifically for recent immigrant students, usually those who have been in the United States for one year or less. The programs are designed primarily for ELLs of high-school age with both language and academic needs, although there are some newcomer schools that also provide services for younger learners. The purpose of these newcomer schools is to offer a safe learning environment for newly arrived older students in order to better meet their particular needs, including literacy development, basic content instruction, basic learning and study skills, and cultural adaptation to school and the United States (Faltis & Coulter, 2008; Olsen, 2000; Short, 2002a). The goal is to accelerate the English language learning of these students while providing immediate access to content instruction and intensive literacy training.

Newcomer programs first came into existence in the late 1970s. Since that time, more than 115 secondary newcomer programs have been documented in more than 29 states (Boyson & Short, 2003). Some school districts have more than one newcomer program. New York City, for example, which has a very large ELL population, has several independent newcomer schools in the different boroughs.

Some newcomer programs may be full day and others half day. Some newcomer high schools are associated with and guarantee admission to a community college upon successful completion of the newcomer program (Constantino & Lavandenz, 1993).

Newcomer programs may be located in separate facilities or established within a traditional high school. The programs may be totally self-contained, with immigrant students staying together for a whole day in classes created to address their unique needs. The program can also be a pull-out program, where students stay for a half day or take two or three newcomer program classes while spending the rest of the day in classes with the mainstream student population.

There are several major benefits to newcomer programs. First, a newcomer program offers a friendlier learning environment with reduced anxiety and stress than a traditional high school. Newly immigrated students feel more at home when they find that they have peers who are also recent immigrants facing similar difficulties with language and culture. This encourages the development of a learning community in which students care about each other's learning and progress, because they are confronting similar issues in the adjustment process.

Second, a newcomer program provides a culturally sensitive learning environment with greater understanding and empathy from the teachers. Teachers and support staff in newcomer programs have received special training in working with ELLs, and with SLIFE in particular; thus, they have a better understanding of the students' academic and affective needs during their adjustment to a new culture, new learning experience, and new language (Chang, 1990; Henze & Lucas, 1993). As a result they are better able to create an appropriate learning environment based on ESL methodology and scaffolded learning, to provide requisite support services, and to tailor the curriculum to students' particular needs.

Major criticisms of newcomer programs tend to focus on issues of segregation of ELLs and the inferior education that may result from isolation (Faltis & Coulter, 2008). According to some ELL educators, such programs often suffer from inadequate support and funding, and are likely to create linguistic isolation, social isolation, labeling, and inequality because ELLs are isolated from their English-speaking peer students (Feinberg, 2000; Friedlander, 1991).

Some of these concerns are not totally unfounded, but as long as school administrators make sure that ELLs enrolled in the newcomer program get ample time in coursework with native English–speaking students and that multilingual multiculturalism is being promoted in the school, potential weaknesses of the newcomer program can be overcome.

Resource Tip

A key resource on newcomer programs is available at www.cal.org/projects/newcomer. html.

The Pull-Out Model

In a pull-out program, SLIFE are taken out of mainstream classes to attend special sessions focused on their particular needs. They meet elsewhere with an ESL teacher, usually in another classroom, an area in the library, or some other designated space. The main features of this model are:

- Classes integrate ESL, academic skills development—including literacy skills—and content area support.
- SLIFE generally spend most of the academic day attending mainstream classes. Only a small portion of the school-day schedule is allocated to ESL classes.
- Teachers coordinate with the school principal and scheduling personnel to arrange schedules and space that maximize the attendance of SLIFE in mainstream academic content classes.

SCHEDULING POSSIBILITIES FOR PULL-OUT SLIFE CLASSES

- Offer classes during the lunch period. Schools may provide a free bag lunch as an additional incentive.
- Offer an English support class that includes focused literacy skills development during the regular mainstream English language arts class.
- Offer the option of substituting a special credit-bearing class as an elective for SLIFE.

Exactly how a pull-out program is structured will depend on the school, the curriculum, scheduling flexibility, available space, and the needs of the particular SLIFE population at that school.

The pull-out model is perhaps best used in schools where SLIFE speak a variety of different languages; this situation precludes their taking part in bilingual or dual-language programs. This type of program does not require that teachers of SLIFE be bilingual or have knowledge of the representative languages. However, it does require that they have a thorough and professional understanding of second language acquisition, ESL approaches, and literacy strategies relevant to ESL classroom practices.

When SLIFE are pulled out of classes for ESL instruction, certain issues must be carefully considered. Pulling out SLIFE may interfere with academic classes and/or make it difficult for these students to take electives. Sometimes, pulling SLIFE out means they must give up lunch or another free period, reducing opportunities for them to socialize with their extended peer groups. Additionally, the loss of lunch period or a free period may be stressful for SLIFE if they depend on that time to complete assignments from other classes or to meet with peers to complete group projects.

Due to the potentially negative aspects of the pull-out model, it has been criticized by some as being the least effective model for language learning (Duke & Mabbot, 2001; Ovando & Collier, 1998). However, pull-out programs can work if their focus is on teaching English and literacy through academic content and not solely on linguistic skills. Successful pull-out programs concentrate on the development of higher-level thinking skills and cognitive abilities, have fully committed and trained teachers and staff, and incorporate careful planning and coordination on the part of teachers and the administration. In addition, successful pull-out programs include the features listed.

ESSENTIAL FEATURES OF SUCCESSFUL PULL-OUT PROGRAMS

- **Extended (60–70 minutes minimum) targeted instruction per day.** SLIFE work in small groups with different teachers to whom they are assigned according to English proficiency level. If more than one group is meeting and teachers do not have their own classrooms, the communal area should be delineated into separate spaces by mobile chalkboards or walls to separate the groups.

- **Individual portfolios.** SLIFE have individual academic portfolios that readily permit the teachers and individual students to track academic progress and identify areas that require more focus from students (see Chapter 7).

- **Flexibility.** SLIFE move from one teacher and group to another depending on progress and needs. Such movement is independent of marking periods or terms.

- **Attending mainstream classes.** SLIFE are exposed to content instruction with the rest of their grades throughout the rest of the school day.

- **Team teaching.** ESL teachers and content area teachers work together to plan lessons that focus on language development through content material for SLIFE.

- **Required after-school program for SLIFE.** SLIFE engage in individual work with teachers, aides, and community and/or honor student tutors to review content material as they simultaneously build basic skills.

The Push-In Model

The push-in model, also known as the inclusion model, retains SLIFE in mainstream classes. Trained ESL teachers and/or bilingual professionals work with SLIFE in the regularly scheduled classes. These specially trained teachers help the mainstream content area teachers modify academic content to make it more comprehensible and accessible to SLIFE. Push-in teachers circulate among the SLIFE to provide additional help and may also work with small groups of students who have difficulty under-standing the content.

The primary advantages of the push-in model are twofold. First, the push-in model exposes SLIFE to the mainstream curriculum, developing students' content knowl-edge and academic language proficiency simultaneously. Even if initial comprehen-sion is minimal, SLIFE at least begin to understand the academic expectations. Another advantage of the push-in model is that this approach helps integrate SLIFE into the student body rather than marginalizing them for participation in "special instruction."

The push-in model is most often found in content area classrooms, such as math, science, and social studies. This model provides an excellent opportunity for team teaching by pairing ESL teachers with content area teachers:

- ESL teachers can work with their mainstream colleagues on different ESL methods and techniques for making content area instruction more accessible to SLIFE.
- ESL teachers of SLIFE draw on concrete texts from mainstream curriculum to include in the objectives for these students.
- Collaborative efforts such as these provide excellent opportunities for task-oriented and group-learning projects across content areas and ESL classes.

The success of this model depends on several factors. Push-in ESL teachers must not be regarded as aides but rather as colleagues on equal footing with the mainstream teachers. In some classes, we have seen the ESL teachers' roles reduced to that of inter-preter or tutor, which is not the intention of the push-in model. In a successful push-in program, the ESL teacher and mainstream teacher each contribute equally in their respective areas of expertise. The ESL teacher contributes knowledge of ESL teach-ing strategies and techniques and the processes of second language acquisition; the mainstream teacher contributes knowledge of content material. Both the mainstream teacher and the ESL teacher work as a team to articulate content and pedagogy and to plan and exchange ideas.

Success is also dependent upon flexibility of scheduling to support team-teach-ing efforts. If there is no regularly scheduled time allotted for ESL teachers and main-stream teachers to coordinate and plan their lessons, it will be difficult for them to integrate purposeful ESL instruction into the mainstream content topics, and as a result, instruction becomes fragmented.

An example of a successful push-in model from one of the high schools we have observed is given.

ONE SUCCESSFUL PUSH-IN MODEL

- **Parallel teaching.** The class is divided according to levels of English language profi-ciency and literacy skills. Native speakers and proficient non-native speakers form one group. Lower-proficiency ELLs form another group, and SLIFE form a third group. Each group receives the content simultaneously, but the language is adjusted according to proficiency level. Additional support materials are used with SLIFE and, if necessary, other ELLs to build missing background content knowledge.

Extended-Day, After-School, and Saturday Models

Extended-day, after-school, and Saturday models serve SLIFE outside of normal school hours. These models generally allow for flexibility in format and content and are geared toward the individual needs of SLIFE. These programs also offer opportunities to make greater use of peer tutors and community volunteers. Some schools offer community service credit to their honor students for assisting in programs for SLIFE.

Extended-Day Programs

The purpose of an extended-day program is to provide students with opportunities to compensate for lost and/or inadequate learning time and/or take elective classes. Extended-day programs include classes for SLIFE, as well as classes available to all students. Usually these programs are class hours added to the existing school schedule; that is, classes are an extension of the regular school day. For example, the bell rings at 2:40 to signal the end of Period 8. Students in extended-day programs proceed to Period 9 classes, while the other students are dismissed. SLIFE proceed to their classes; other students proceed to elective classes such as art, dance, or music. These classes are considered part of the school day and are credit-bearing in an effort to help students complete the requisite studies and graduate within an acceptable time span. SLIFE classes are not considered remedial; a standard curriculum is followed, school-designated textbooks are used, and classes are taught by certified teachers.

After-School Programs

After-school programs are exactly that: programs that take place after regularly scheduled classes have ended for the day, rather than extensions of the regular school day. The sessions focus on literacy, language, and/or content area topics. SLIFE receive no credit toward graduation and the classes do not necessarily follow standard curriculum. These programs are similar to tutoring programs but with more organization and structure. SLIFE work individually or in small groups with teachers, aides, community volunteers, and/or honors students.

Depending on the number of SLIFE participating in the after-school program, students can be assigned to different groups and rotate among teachers for different types of instruction. To ensure that SLIFE understand schedules, each student has his or her schedule cards detailing assigned sessions. Each day at the beginning of the session, students pull out their schedule cards from a box, go to their assigned sessions, and rotate in groups according to the time schedule. SLIFE can also engage in supplemental work on a computer station during any given session; however, for computer activities to be effective, students must be closely supervised. A sample schedule is provided below to give a clearer picture of how this works.

SAMPLE AFTER-SCHOOL SCHEDULE

Students are assigned to different groups, depending on language proficiency. Students stay in one group for 35–40 minutes and then rotate.

Time	Group 1	Group 2	Group 3
2:30 – 3:10	ESL/Reading	Math, Science, Technology	Art & Literacy
3:15 – 3:55	Art & Literacy	ESL/Reading	Math, Science, Technology
4:00 – 4:40	Math, Science, Technology	Art & Literacy	ESL/Reading

Saturday Programs

Saturday programs are similar to after-school programs in terms of structure and purpose, but they are more likely to include parents/guardians. In some of these programs, parents/guardians attend the same classes as SLIFE. Others offer separate classes for parents/guardians, including basic literacy, ESL, computer literacy, or parenting/life skills. Childcare is often provided to encourage mothers—and/or SLIFE who would otherwise be responsible for caring for younger siblings—to participate in Saturday programs. Students who are not SLIFE and help with childcare receive community service hours. Saturday programs may offer additional enrichment activities such as ESL instruction through music, dance, or drama; often they include field trips as part of their curriculum and planning.

Especially popular and successful after-school and Saturday programs we have seen are those that offer classes in newspaper-based literacy, website design, and Adobe Photoshop.

Newspaper-based literacy. In this class, SLIFE learn to understand and read the different parts of newspapers, chosen either by the teacher or by the students. They compare writing styles, approaches to news, and types of information included. Students write summaries and reflections and share their comments with other SLIFE. They maintain portfolios of newspaper clippings along with their own and their classmates' commentaries.

Resource Tip

News for You is an easy-to-read weekly newspaper written for adult ESL students. See this website: www.news-for-you.com.

For less proficient SLIFE, teachers provide sentence patterns or frames, like those shown, to help them complete their writing.

SAMPLE SENTENCE FRAMES

- I agree with _____ because _____.
- I disagree with _____because _____.
- I don't understand this piece because _____.
- I liked what _____ wrote about _____
  because _____.
- I didn't like what _____ wrote about _____
  because _____.
- This piece was interesting because _____.

Using the Internet and learning Web design. SLIFE, like most students, are fascinated by technology. Using the Internet and learning Web design help SLIFE develop their language, literacy, and content-area knowledge in addition to promoting their creativity. Using these technology-related activities also gives SLIFE a strong sense of accomplishment—a feeling they may not experience in their content-area classes. SLIFE often find that the computer allows them to be more creative and more productive than if they were writing and/or drawing by hand. By using the Internet for research, students become familiar with search engines such as Google, learning how to enter search words to get the information they need and how to read, interpret, and use the text they find.

For Web design, SLIFE work with software to create Web pages. This requires planning (Web pages are often sketched out with pencil on paper before putting them on the computer); organization (users must be able to follow directions in an ordered sequence); manipulation of text; creative manipulation of photographs and other graphics; and the generation of original illustrations and designs. These productions can be "edited" by the ESL teacher and used as a basis for whole-class lessons. Finally, they are uploaded to the Web where they can be displayed as an accomplishment. They may even serve as a means of communicating with friends still living in their home country.

There are two different kinds of Web pages that students work with. SLIFE use preformatted (pre-coded in html) pages where all they have to do is supply text, photos, drawings, and other materials. More proficient and technologically advanced SLIFE learn and use html to create the way the final page will appear.

Web design is integrated into many different types of lessons, whether ESL, history, science, or English Language Arts. Students can design Web pages based on a field trip, such as Historic Lower Manhattan, or on more personal topics like "My New Life in the United States" or "Who Am I?" More academic topics can include pages based on, for example, science topics such as, "What Is a Cell?"

Teachers "edit" student work by providing oral feedback on both the content and design of the Web page. Before any page is uploaded to the Internet, the teacher and student carefully edit it for correct text and test any live buttons, drop-down menus, and other features to make sure that they work.

Practical Considerations

Extended day, after-school, and Saturday programs frequently rely on teacher aides, volunteers, and/or Computer Assisted Language Learning (CALL) to support the learning of SLIFE. It is important to use all available resources to best serve the needs of these students. However, trained teachers must be present to structure, coordinate, and supervise activities to ensure that the focus remains on academic language development through content and that programs do not become mere tutorials. We have seen too many instances where this is the case and where programs are disorganized and/or inadequate to meet the learning needs of SLIFE. This seemed to be a relatively common shortcoming with the use of CALL programs when students were working with software language programs in a computer lab. The only person available to help the students was the computer lab assistant—not a qualified ESL instructor who could explain language questions and mistakes and offer necessary help. There must be careful planning and coordination to ensure that the program is well organized and well structured, that work is not purely remedial, and that teachers use a standard curriculum. Successful programs have clear, realistic goals and objectives.

From the students' perspective, these three programs, which all take place outside the regular school day, are likely to be viewed as "extra" and not something to be taken all that seriously. Family responsibilities, the need to work, or similar obligations may come first in their minds. School administrators and teachers must help SLIFE and their parents/guardians fully understand the goals and objectives of the program the school provides. SLIFE are less likely to participate in these learning opportunities without their parents'/guardians' understanding of what these programs offer and why attendance is important.

None of these programs should be remedial. While SLIFE need the extra time to work on their literacy skills, academic English proficiency, and content knowledge, these programs can give students opportunities to develop interests and skills in other areas.

One way to encourage SLIFE participation is to allow students to earn at least partial credit toward academic classes. Again, a program must have a careful learning plan with quality supervision. In addition, when schools offer high-interest classes, SLIFE are more likely to make attendance a priority.

In order to make up for lost time and to meet high school graduation requirements, SLIFE need more time and more support. The flexible scheduling that characterizes the newcomer programs and permits up to four hours of additional language classes is a model that should be carefully considered by schools with a significant population of SLIFE. The push-in and pull-out programs can also be used as effective means to reach SLIFE, provided that staff have been adequately trained to deal with

the multiple facets of these programs. Carefully constructed and coordinated programs can make excellent use of the time allocated by the school clock, but still more
is needed.

Just as most of us feel that there are not enough hours in a given day, the academic day also falls short of the number of hours needed for SLIFE. Extended-day,
after-school, and Saturday programs are possible ways to find more time to assist
SLIFE. To be effective, these programs need to be structured to help SLIFE develop
English language proficiency and literacy skills, further their knowledge of grade-
level content subject matter. Through these programs, SLIFE should develop creative
outlets and learn to use tools, such as computers, that will ease their transitions into
the post-secondary school world.

**ESSENTIAL ELEMENTS OF SUCCESSFUL
EXTENDED-DAY, AFTER-SCHOOL, AND SATURDAY PROGRAMS**

- Clear goals and objectives are established.

- Goals and objectives are not limited to areas in which students are deficient; programs include activities that allow them to develop higher-level thinking skills and
personal interests.

- Learning activities should not only include more formal learning but should also
take advantage of the less-crowded space in the school building to allow more
group work, individual learning, hands-on activities, computer and science labs, and
projects.

- Field trips are open to parent/guardian participation.

- Dedicated staff and teachers are involved in these programs not for the extra pay but
because they truly want to help SLIFE.

Chapter 5

Overview of Approaches and Practices

THIS CHAPTER REVIEWS THE MOST ESSENTIAL APPROACHES AND BEST PRACTICES FOR TEACHING SLIFE that we have observed. In the following chapter, we will focus on some of the most promising activities for SLIFE.

Many essential approaches and best practices have been identified for ELLs, all of which are even more important for their potential application to SLIFE. As we have seen in previous chapters, these students have specific needs and require additional support. In choosing which practice or practices to adopt for SLIFE, teachers should give careful consideration to the makeup of the school's student population, curriculum requirements, the degree of available administrative support, and other realities of the school system in which they work. Regardless of how academic content and English proficiency classes are organized, there are components essential to all classroom practices and applicable to all SLIFE, no matter what their linguistic backgrounds.

Freeman & Freeman (2003) suggest that there are four essential keys to academic success for this population. First, students must be engaged in a theme-based curriculum that is challenging. Too often ELLs, and SLIFE even more so, are not given appropriate and requisite access to content-area instruction (Rubinstein-Ávila, 2003; Valdés, 2001). Second, teachers need to draw on students' backgrounds. SLIFE come to school with myriad life experiences and concrete, real-world skills, and abilities or "funds of knowledge" (Gonzáles & Amati, 1997; Moll et al., 1992), which teachers can and should incorporate into students' learning experiences (Xu, 2003). Third, teachers need to plan and promote collaborative activities and use scaffolded instruction. Collaborative activities encourage students to work together and are consistent with their collectivistic orientation, allowing them to build and maintain personal relationships and to draw knowledge and learn from one another (Marshall, 1998; Vygotsky, 1978). Collaborative activities also encourage students to develop a sense of individual responsibility by giving each person responsibility for a specific task (DeCapua & Marshall, forthcoming). Fourth, students need to develop confidence in their ability to become capable learners who value schooling.

It is necessary to emphasize once again that SLIFE need more of everything: more time to learn, more patience from educators, more language and content modifications, and greater understanding of their needs as high-context, collectivistic learners from cultures with a pragmatic worldview. For many SLIFE, basic concepts and fundamental skills need to be developed and reinforced. For this to work best, learning should be positive, open, and experiential. SLIFE must have plentiful opportunities to participate actively in classroom activities that allow them to develop language, literacy, and content knowledge through multiple intelligences (Gardner, 1983/2003). Active participation consists of involvement that is goal oriented, with clearly stated language and content objectives, steps to be accomplished, and assessment elements, for both student and teacher.

Because SLIFE are often unfamiliar with, and thus uncomfortable in structured school environments, they often have short attention spans and need to be physically engaged in learning. Total Physical Response (TPR) (Asher, 1982) emphasizes the use of physical activity as an integral tool for language learning. To redirect restiveness, teachers can prepare lessons incorporating TPR that include physical activity rather than having SLIFE sitting and working at a desk with pencil and paper for long stretches of time. Teachers should plan lessons, so SLIFE "do" things rather than only read, listen, and write. In a SLIFE math lesson, a teacher can, for example, have students build models to represent fractions.

The teacher first assigns the students to small groups. Each group is given a different kind of material to work with, such as a sheet of paper or a piece of rope. One group, for example, is given a yard-long piece of rope but not told how long it is. The students must measure the rope to determine its length. Next, they must determine the three equal parts. They will then mark the rope off into three sections, each one foot (12 inches) long, and will show their findings to the rest of the class. With this activity, they learn to work with feet and inches and learn the concept of one-third (1/3) of something. After, they write a short paragraph explaining what they did.

Resource Tip

The classic book on TPR is James J. Asher's *Learning Another Language Through Actions: The Complete Teacher's Guidebook,* published by Sky Oaks Productions, Los Gatos, CA, 1982.

This website features articles, resources, and other useful information related to TPR: www.tpr-world.com/.

Bloom's Taxonomy

Successful instruction of SLIFE simultaneously develops a student's language proficiency, literacy skills, content-area knowledge, and academic worldview. Teachers need to think about how the approaches, practices, and specific activities discussed here promote development in all of these areas, while also meeting the affective needs of SLIFE. With this in mind, it is useful to review Bloom's Taxonomy of Educational Objectives, originally proposed in 1956, as shown on page 54.

FIGURE 4: Bloom's Taxonomy

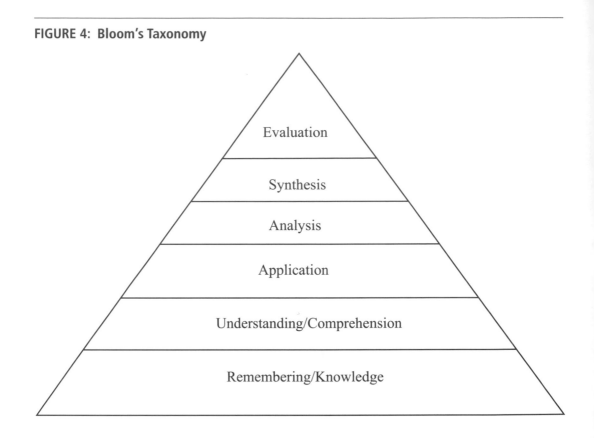

Bloom's taxonomy represents a hierarchy of cognitive skills. The six major categories represent increasing levels of complexity in ascending order. The higher one goes in the pyramid, the higher the level of abstraction and the more demanding the cognitive task. Students must master the lower levels in order to engage in the higher ones. For true learning to take place, they must go beyond the lower levels and learn to engage in higher-order thinking skills.

Bloom's taxonomy is often used as a guide for hierarchizing the types of questions used by teachers to test students' knowledge. The lower levels focus on "display" questions—that is, questions about literal knowledge where the answer is obvious and there are a limited number of possible responses. Such questions include "What is the title of the book?" or "Who gave the Gettysburg Address?" The higher up one goes in the hierarchy, the more abstract the level of teachers' questions becomes, requiring various levels of cognitive thinking and more complex responses. At these levels, questions are usually more in the order of "Why did the Roman Catholic church condemn Galileo's astronomical findings?" or "Why is *zero* important to mathematics?"

Too often, learning in any classroom is focused on the bottom levels of the pyramid (Gall, 1984). In our experience, teachers of SLIFE who did not merely focus on the lower levels of Bloom's taxonomy are the ones that facilitated the most growth and development among their students. Through careful lesson planning, scaffolding, and extensive group and cooperative learning, SLIFE can develop the higher-level skills and their academic worldviews.

This chart provides key verbs and sample types of questions related to Bloom's categories of educational objectives. Using this hierarchy as a guide, teachers of SLIFE can gradually develop lesson objectives and lesson materials that include not only the lower levels (remembering/knowledge; understanding/comprehension) but those that also address the higher-order thinking skills.

KEY VERBS AND EDUCATIONAL OBJECTIVES

Evaluation	Can the student justify a stand or decision? Key verbs: *argue, defend, judge, select, support, value, evaluate, assess, rate, predict*	Which Constitutional Amendment do you think is the most important and why?
Synthesis	Can the student put together ideas into a unique product?	How might the world be different if Great Britain had defeated the American revolutionaries?
Analysis	Can the student distinguish between the different parts? Key verbs: *compare, contrast, critique, distinguish, examine, experiment, question, test*	After studying World War I and World War II, what can you conclude about the claim that both wars were really one war?
Application	Can the student use information in a new way? Key verbs: *choose, demonstrate, dramatize, employ, illustrate, report, interpret, operate, solve, use, show*	Based on our studies of different political systems, how would you classify the following nations?
Understanding/ Comprehension	Can the student explain ideas or concepts? Key verbs: *classify, describe, discuss, explain, identify, locate, recognize, select, translate, paraphrase, generalize, summarize*	Explain *photosynthesis*. Discuss the Bill of Rights.
Knowledge/ Remembering	Can the student recall or remember the information? Key verbs: *tell, define, name, list, memorize, recall, repeat, arrange, duplicate, state*	What is the capital of the United States? Who was the first president of the United States? What were the Articles of Confederation?

Small-Group/Cooperative Learning

> Small group is better and I learning more because in big
> class I can no understand; I can no ask questions, can no
> raise my hand. Small everyone talk, explain and we ask ques-
> tion each other and teacher. I learn a lot, especially science.
>   —Rosa

Small-group or cooperative learning, important for all ELLs (Holt, 1993), is essential for SLIFE. Small groups allow teachers to provide SLIFE with differentiated, targeted instruction, greater scaffolding, and to engage more of them in community learning. Small groups encourage cooperative learning where students learn from each other as they complete assigned tasks. Cooperative learning promotes the use of activities that encourage a collective effort among SLIFE to achieve group goals while holding students individually accountable for their contributions in achieving these goals (Calderón, 1990; Davidson, 1990; Slavin, 1995). Moreover, by cooperating with each other, SLIFE can take on more complex tasks than they could working on their own because they are tapping into each other's knowledge and strengths. Students learn by observing and implementing the strategies of their peers (Cazden, 1986; Vygotsky, 1978).

Small groups provide SLIFE with more opportunities to interact with one another and with their teacher, and to practice, ask questions, and stay on task. Interaction is critical in supporting students' language learning, academic achievement, and social and affective development.

Resource Tip

"Cooperative Learning in the Secondary School: Maximizing Language Acquisition, Academic Achievement, and Social Development," by D. Holt, B. Chips, and D. Wallace, provides an excellent overview, complete with examples of cooperative learning for ELLs at the secondary level in different subject areas. The authors provide excellent diagrams and charts for cooperative learning that can be further adapted to meet the needs of SLIFE. Available at www.ncela.gwu.edu/pubs/pigs/pig12.htm.

As small groups permit more student talk and less teacher-fronted discourse, they provide more opportunities for meaningful interaction among SLIFE. Meaningful interaction is central to the development of language proficiency (Ellis, 1984; Mackey, 1999). As students negotiate meaning to effectively communicate with others, they begin to recognize (explicitly or implicitly) the language forms that make them comprehensible to their listeners. The give-and-take of natural conversation presents students with opportunities to focus their attention on specific areas of language that may be causing breakdowns in communication (Gass, 1997; Long, 1996). Meaningful interactions allow students to become actively involved in the language learning process in a way that teacher centered-instruction does not provide.

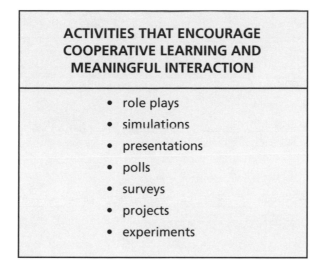

ACTIVITIES THAT ENCOURAGE COOPERATIVE LEARNING AND MEANINGFUL INTERACTION

- role plays
- simulations
- presentations
- polls
- surveys
- projects
- experiments

Teachers need to practice careful management to ensure that all SLIFE are learning and participating equally in their small groups. To be most effective, group size should be limited to no more than six students; the ideal number is four. Group tasks must be well structured with each student assigned a task to accomplish; the task should be clearly defined, with specific steps provided, if applicable. A worksheet like the one on page 58 can help guide SLIFE and keep them on task for longer, more involved assignments.

Sample Framework for Group Work

Start date/time:	End date/time:
Assignment:	Students:

Unit/Theme/Reading:

Essential Questions:

Content Objective:

Language Objective:

Thinking Objective:

Product:

Reflection and Evaluation

+ What I liked What I learned	**−** What I didn't like What I want or need to learn

Experiential Learning: Field Trips

Field trips are key elements of effective experiential learning for SLIFE. Such trips expand learning about U.S. culture beyond the classrooms, connect textbook content with real-life situations, take advantage of the rich resources around school districts, and provide SLIFE with rich experiential learning. Field trips also provide excellent opportunities to include parents/guardians in school activities. Parents/guardians can be invited to help chaperone trips and benefit from the outings as much as the students.

> Today I with my after school classmates took the bus to walking New York City of around Manhattan.
>   In the bus I saw many big buildings. I like United Nations. There are 195 flags in front of the United Nations building. It means 195 countries. Central park is big and huge, full of trees and people.
>   We also passed 34th Street. I saw Empire State building and Madison square garden. The Empire State building is the tallest building in New York City now.
>   We also visited St John Divine Church. I took a picture and made a pray for my parents and friends.
>   —Blanca

> I saw so many different parts when we go trip. It opens my eyes to a lot of things.
>   —Seong

In order to be effective as learning tools, field trips must be carefully planned, relevant to both the larger curriculum and to the specific learning needs of SLIFE, and have clearly defined goals and objectives. These trips should be more than "just for fun." Furthermore, successful field trips tie into task-based and project-based learning with pre- and post-trip learning activities such as:

Pre-trip activities:
- general information session about the field trip destination to develop students' background knowledge of the destination, including brochures, PowerPoint presentations, and DVDs
- short readings related to the field trip destination
- initial planning of individual projects for post-trip follow-up

Trip activities:
- note-taking (on overnight field trips students can engage in journal writing)
- video recording
- photography

Post-trip activities:

- written narratives and/or recorded oral narratives on the trip, including essays and poems
- PowerPoint presentations (small group or individual) for other students and parents/guardians
- preparation of exhibits or displays on school bulletin boards
- presentation of student work on school website

Differentiated Learning

Although the terms *differentiated learning* and *indiviudalized learning* are at times used interchangeably, they mean very different things. Differentiated learning focuses on the adaptation of curriculum content and ways of learning content for groups or clusters of students at approximately the same skills level. Differentiated learning acknowledges that there are multiple intelligences, that different students learn in different ways (Gardner, 1983/2003), and that they tend to "cluster" or group together within approximate developmental ranges or according to types of learning needs and learning styles. Individualized instruction, on the other hand, attempts to address the learning needs and learning style of each individual student—a very difficult and unrealistic approach for teachers faced with the diverse needs of many students in their classrooms. Because differentiation focuses on clusters of learners, it serves as a more realistic framework for teachers than individualized instruction.

Resource Tips

"Different Strokes for Little Folks: Carol Ann Tomlinson on Differentiated Instruction," by Carol Bafile (2004), discusses in detail the difference between differentiated learning and individualized instruction. The article also provides links to additional articles. Available at www.educationworld.com/a_issues/chat/chat107.shtml.

The ASCD website below offers numerous books, lesson plans, professional development manuals, and other materials on differentiated instruction. Although this website is not geared specifically toward ELLs or SLIFE, the information provides valuable information and resources that can be adapted: www.ascd.org.

Scaffolding Instruction

Cazden (1988) suggests that scaffolding is an essential element in helping students become independent learners. Although Cazden does not make mention of ELLs or SLIFE, the notion of scaffolding is most certainly applicable to these learners. As it implies, scaffolding refers to temporary structures that are put in place to help build larger, more solid and longer lasting structures. Similar to the wooden or metal supports used in the construction of buildings, classroom scaffolding consists of strategies used by teachers to empower students, so they can become successful and independent learners. Scaffolding provides SLIFE with the support they need to develop skills and knowledge, until ultimately they are able to understand and to find solutions on their own. In other words, as SLIFE become more knowledgeable and more competent, scaffolds or support are gradually removed. This approach asks that teachers assess the kind of support SLIFE need to ultimately help themselves and to move on to the next challenge or task.

Initially, teachers provide a great deal of support to SLIFE to help them access content that might otherwise be beyond their levels. The teacher's role is to provide considerable, lesson-specific support to aid students' understanding and learning. This support may include strategies such as modeling; contextualization of content and language; and use of TPR, visuals, and realia. As students' abilities and knowledge develop, teachers gradually withdraw this support until the students become independent learners, that is, learners who are capable of knowing how to approach new material and access it on their own.

For example, high school students are often required to read one or more plays by Shakespeare as part of general English language arts (ELA) requirements. Native speakers of English and ELA-proficient ELLs read the plays in original Elizabethan English. When working with SLIFE, however, teachers can use a Shakespeare series designed especially for non-native speakers of English and geared to 16–18 year olds. The vocabulary has been simplified, but the books have excellent notes, glossaries, and resources that serve a wide range of academic language abilities. Teachers will need to carefully scaffold each lesson; however, additional resources are available for modeling—for example, a variety of commercially available films (DVDs), which can be shown to the students and then used by them as a reference as they proceed (at their own pace) scene by scene through the text. Having students act out scenes gets them actively involved in the text as they become more familiar with the language—meaning, pronunciation, speech rhythms, and so on. It may take longer to get through a Shakespeare play with SLIFE, but when SLIFE are aware that they are studying the same text as mainstream students, they feel less isolated and more competent.

TYPES OF SCAFFOLDS

Contextualization	Embed new vocabulary, concepts, and content in a sensory environment (e.g., pictures, videos, objects) to make them more comprehensible to the learner
Modeling	Demonstrate the process and show the end result (e.g., a completed graphic organizer, sample letter); model phrases, sentence structures, etc.
Connecting	Establish links to other material (e.g., previously learned vocabulary, concepts, and content)
Schema Building	Show different types of relationships among concepts and content (e.g., semantic maps, sequence diagrams, classifications, graphic organizers)
Metacognition	Reflect on thinking (e.g., oral/written reflections, journals, self-evaluations)

Chapter 6 presents specific examples of scaffolds, such as graphic organizers and sentence frames.

Project-Based Learning

Project-based learning is grounded in the belief that successful learning is interactive and participatory and provides student autonomy in and responsibility for learning (Wilson & Cole, 1991); it is motivating, stimulating, empowering, and challenging and can be adapted for any ability level (Harris & Katz, 2001). Learning activities are authentic, designed to promote student interest and motivation; that is, students learn content-area material and apply what they have learned to real-world situations (Fletcher, 2007). Project-based learning encourages students to find interdisciplinary connections as they explore subject matter and supports the development of different language skills through exploration of content material. Project-based learning emphasizes both process and product, while encouraging collaborative and independent work that support the development of cognitive skills. Experiential learning, exploration, and application are essential components. As many different tools as possible are used for learning, whether book and text sources, computer technology, art, field-based investigations, or other resources.

THE TEN BASIC STEPS OF PROJECT-BASED LEARNING
1. Determining a theme
2. Identifying the final outcome
3. Structuring the project
4. Preparing students for the language needs of Step 5
5. Collecting data
6. Preparing students for the language needs of Step 7

7. Compiling and analyzing data
8. Preparing students for language needs of Step 9
9. Presenting the project
10. Evaluating the project

(Stoller, 2002, p. 112)

Observed end products of project-based learning include

- Flyers and brochures
- Wall displays (newspaper clippings)
- Artwork
- Audio-video creations
- PowerPoint presentations
- Web pages and blogs
- Performances (talent shows, café nights)

These are just some of the more successful approaches and practices used with ELLs and adapted for use with SLIFE that we have seen. There are others that teachers, administrators, and relevant school personnel may wish to explore in terms of possible adaptation for their respective schools. As SLIFE have only recently come into the spotlight, there are not yet any long-term studies examining the validity of such practices and their outcomes. When adapting an approach for the classroom, teachers should be familiar with the practice to ensure that it is appropriate for their students and that it can be adapted to the particular needs of SLIFE.

Case Study: Project-Based Learning Overnight Field Trip

Nature

Clouds decorates blue sky
Green grass calms morning sunshine
Leaves stretch out of tree branches
Back to nature my heart flies

—Dong

This poem was written by a SLIFE after participating in a project-based learning experience that included an overnight field trip. The unit focus was on environmental studies and involved close collaboration among all of the teachers in the related content areas, as well ESL teachers. Students of all classes, not only SLIFE, were involved in the trip, with teachers providing additional learning support and modified activities for SLIFE. An outline of this field trip experience and project-based learning unit follows on page 64.

Sample Project-Based Learning Model:
Trip to a Local Environmental Education Center and Projects on Environmental Studies

Pre-trip activities:

- Orientation to Environmental Studies (all content classes cover related subject material)
- Forming project groups; establishing tasks; reviewing objectives, goals, and steps to complete projects

Trip activities:

Day One

Morning	Afternoon	Evening
Arrive at environmental center	Outdoor living skills (crossing a polluted river, survival skills, etc.)	Night hiking
Orientation in groups	Action socialization and field study in the woods (study of animals, ponds, bird prey, protection of birds, etc.)	Campfire
	Students take photos for later writing project	

Day Two

Morning & Afternoon	Evening
Mountain hiking (learning about wildlife, safety skills; making fires, putting up tents, building shelter, etc.)	Games and singing

Day Three

Summary and Depart for School

Post-trip activities

- Group and individual work
  - Newspaper. Students prepare a newspaper with articles about the trip. In addition to their own stories, they interview other students and teachers about the experience.
    - Skills required: interviewing, reading, writing
  - Photo writing. Students choose one of the photos they took on the trip and write about it. The writing format can be a reflection, story, or poem. Students can also use Adobe Photoshop to edit photographs.
    - Skills required: reading, writing, computer literacy (e.g., knowledge of Microsoft Word, Adobe Photoshop)

Chapter 6

Best Classroom Techniques

IN TEACHING SLIFE, TEACHERS WILL WANT TO REMEMBER THAT SCHOOL AND EDUCATIONAL EXPEC-tations are, in large part, unfamiliar and different experiences for this population. In general, as members of high-context, collectivistic cultures with pragmatic world-views, SLIFE will have learning priorities and paradigms that differ from those of the U.S. educational system. The kind of knowledge considered to be important in the context of U.S. classrooms may not be valued in the same way by SLIFE. Given these different perspectives, teachers must continually identify for SLIFE the important elements of each and every learning situation, as well as those details that are less critical. Teachers should also keep in mind that different content areas, such as science, history, or math, have their own content-specific vocabularies, discourse styles, and different ways of organizing and presenting material. In order to have a thorough understanding of each content area, SLIFE must learn these differences. This chapter offers practical suggestions for teachers and examples of actual classroom practices and procedures we have seen that work particularly well with SLIFE.

Routines

When a teacher establishes clear routines, students know what to expect, which relieves them of the burden of wondering "what's next" and permits them to focus on other areas. If SLIFE know *what* is expected of them and *when*, they can learn how to prioritize the academic demands they face and better determine how to respond to them effectively rather than floundering as they try to understand what they need to do and why. The use of classroom routines does not suggest a lack of creativity or innovative thinking on the part of the teacher but rather simply provides another tool. Routines should be varied but consistent in order to sustain the interests of SLIFE and keep them motivated.

An essential routine is the posting of a daily class schedule. At the beginning of each class session, teachers should post a schedule and review it with the students. For SLIFE who are less-proficient, the teacher will want to include visual reminders of routine components like those on page 66.

FIGURE 5:   Daily Class Schedule for SLIFE

Graphic Organizers

> I like these [graphic organizers] because I can see how I
> suppose to do and what I need learn and what everything
> mean. My small group (ESL) teacher give lots of them and
> other classes, too, not just English class so it's more easy
> than book, which have lots of words and everything I don't
> know.
>
> —Emile

As the name implies, graphic organizers are visual aids that convey essential concepts by way of graphic arrangements of key words, phrases, and sentences, together with other graphic elements such as arrows, boxes, and lines to show relationships among key elements (Ives, 2007). Because graphic organizers reduce the amount of linguistic input while visually emphasizing central concepts and relationships, they are an extremely valuable scaffolding strategy in making content more immediately accessible and comprehensible (Robinson, 1998). There are many types of graphic organizers from which teachers can choose; selection will depend on the concepts, relationships, and subject material that are the focus of a given lesson (see Appendix for examples). As with any other tool, SLIFE will need help and practice in learning how to use graphic organizers; however, we found that once students have grasped the principle behind these organizers, they find them invaluable as a learning tool.

Resource Tip

There are numerous websites that provide free, downloadable graphic organizers, although generally not for ELLs. The following website offers graphic organizers developed by ESL teacher Judie Haynes specifically for ELLs, which can easily be used with SLIFE: www.everythingesl.net/inservices/graphic_organizers.php.

Choral Poetry Reading

Teachers can build on the experience many SLIFE have with oral language discourse by reading poems with their students, particularly the poetry SLIFE are studying in their mainstream ELA classes. We have observed that SLIFE frequently enjoy participating in choral reading, especially if the text has strong rhythms and pronounced rhyme schemes. Choral reading provides them with a chance to appreciate the cadences of poems that are not always fully explored in ELA classes.

The teacher begins the activity by introducing or reviewing key vocabulary as needed, and then reads the selected poem aloud once as SLIFE listen. The teacher reads the poem a second time, as students follow along by pointing to each word on their own copies of the poem as the teacher reads. Alternatively, there is a copy of the poem in the front of the class that is visible to all, and either the teacher or a student points to each word as it is read. After the teacher asks questions and checks for comprehension, the class as a whole reads the poem aloud. Next, the teacher assigns individuals or groups of students different parts to read aloud. For example, girls and boys can alternate lines or stanzas, or students can count off and the odd and even numbers can alternate lines or stanzas. (The teacher might also ask students to suggest other ways of doing choral reading.)

Once SLIFE have practiced this poem several times, the teacher has students form small groups and hands them another poem. (If a poem is very long, the teacher might divide it among several groups, each assigned several stanzas.) The teacher again reads the poem aloud as students first listen and then read along as he or she reads the poem a second time. Each group is then instructed to come up with its own choral reading, to practice it, and then to perform the reading for the rest of the class.

Class Books

Class books serve a number of purposes. They are excellent learning tools for SLIFE because they incorporate the three steps of MALP (see Chapter 3). They can help SLIFE learn to organize a variety of materials, such as maps, photographs, and other documents. Class books, like one shown in Figure 6, teach and reinforce the sequencing of events while encouraging SLIFE to share their personal experiences and cultures and to draw on their individual funds of knowledge. Planning, designing, and creating such books promote the integration of technology (i.e., the use of computers, scanners, software, and so on) into the lessons.

To introduce this project, teachers may want to begin with a reading selection about an immigrant's journey to the United States or have students view a DVD recounting the story of immigrants who entered the United States through New

FIGURE 6: Class Books: Example Autobiography

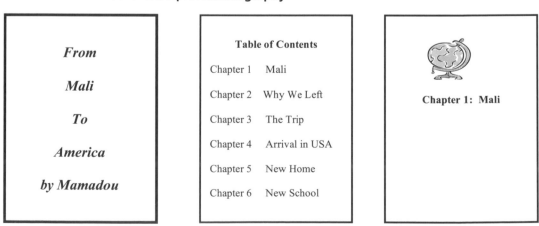

York's Ellis Island. SLIFE can then discuss their own experiences: why they came to the United States and how they did so. Students might next complete a graphic organizer comparing their own immigration experiences with those of immigrants to who arrived through Ellis Island. They can also compare and contrast their experiences with those of their classmates. From this beginning, SLIFE can set to work writing their own books, which can be developed over the course of several weeks or even throughout the school year; students can add new "chapters," covering topics relevant to them—their school work and experiences, their lives outside of school, their families, and so on. SLIFE should be encouraged to incorporate artwork and/or photos in the class books.

Using maps (geography), describing life and events in one's home country (history), and calculating time spent traveling (math) provide opportunities to incorporate other content areas into the ESL classroom. Class books can serve as an assessment tool for teachers in much the same way as a portfolio. The two could even be incorporated. On a more subjective note, they can also serve as a means of helping newly arrived SLIFE maintain their old identities while creating new ones in their current surroundings.

Resource Tip

For resources on immigration to the United States, including stories by immigrants and links to other materials, visit

www.ellisisland.org/
http://teacher.scholastic.com/activities/immigration/index.htm

Autobiography and Biography Collage Project

Although autobiographical collages are not a new idea (e.g., Moskowitz, 1978), like class books, they work especially well with SLIFE because they include the three steps of MALP (see Chapter 3). Autobiographical collages are also very flexible in terms of application to both English and social studies classes, and SLIFE can create them using many different media: books, periodicals, websites, portraits, and PowerPoint presentations.

Part A

Students make collages of pictures that show how they see themselves at different stages of their lives. These pictures can be photos that they have taken themselves, photos from magazines, or photos that they download from the Internet. They can also include their own drawings. They then write words, phrases, and/or sentences that they paste onto the collage. Alternatively, they can make a PowerPoint presentation of who they are and present their work to the rest of the class.

Part B

Students choose (or are assigned) an important personality from their history/social studies text. They prepare a collage or PowerPoint presentation about this person and include a timeline of important events in this person's life.

Class books need not be limited to autobiographies and can be expanded to include other topics, such as the home culture of SLIFE and/or topics from their funds of knowledge; such topics make school learning relevant and personal for students and play an essential role in motivating them (Doherty, Hilberg, Pinal, & Tharp, 2003).

Listening and Reading with Audio Books

Encouraging SLIFE to listen to an audio recording of a story, poem, or a book while they read along is a valuable way to improve both students' listening comprehension and reading skills. This is a type of scaffolding activity in that listening and reading are providing mutual support and reinforcement. Listening while reading along accustoms the ear to the intonation, stress patterns, and rhythm of spoken English. Reading along while listening helps to develop reading decoding skills (e.g., letter, word, and sound correspondence) and pronunciation skills.

There are many commercially produced audio recordings of stories and other readings available on cassette tapes and CDs. Teachers need to be careful that the speaking level on these recordings is appropriate for the proficiency level of the learners. Audio books suitable for children are not necessarily appropriate for SLIFE. Teachers should watch for idioms, colloquialisms, and/or unusual expressions or phrases, and the speed or rate of delivery, as well as regional dialects, that might pose difficulties for SLIFE.

Teachers can also make their own recordings for students. An efficient way to do this is to work with small groups of learners, each supplied with a recording device and the selected reading. Teachers read a story or excerpt aloud while students record the passage(s). Devices such as MP3 players are very useful for activities of this sort and are easily portable. Students can listen to the recorded versions of the text and read the excerpt or story as often as they like. This also allows for differentiated learning as teachers select reading passages appropriate for different proficiency levels and adapt their rates of speaking accordingly.

Vocabulary Books

Student vocabulary books serve various functions. SLIFE, together with their teachers, choose which words they need and want to learn to include in their vocabulary books. Because these are student-generated, SLIFE take ownership and responsibility for the content of their vocabulary books, the visual look of the "book," and how each word is defined. Developing and maintaining their own vocabulary books produces a sense of accomplishment among SLIFE because they have concrete evidence of their individual growth in the mastery of English words.

To create a personal vocabulary book, each SLIFE should have a loose-leaf binder with a tab for each letter of the alphabet. Using loose-leaf binders rather than bound notebooks allows students to add pages as needed. (Using index cards for vocabulary words and filing them in a box is not recommended; it has been our observation that SLIFE, who often have difficulty organizing large amounts of print materials, are put off by this strategy.)

In their vocabulary books, students define words in any way they wish; for example, they may choose to include an English definition, a translation, an illustration, an example of how the word is used in a sentence, or any combination of these approaches, as shown.

Amina's Sample Vocabulary Book Pages

be washed up *Context: After several accidents, the race car driver <u>was washed up</u>.* *Meaning: His career as a driver ended.*	**plot** *Context: The Duke of Buckingham <u>plotted</u> to take the throne from King Henry VII (7th).* *Meaning: made a plan in secret*

Story Development Practice

Another effective learning tool for SLIFE is story development practice. In this activity, the teacher begins by selecting a short reading on a relevant topic. For SLIFE with particularly low English proficiency, this selection may need to be limited to five to eight sentences. After previewing key vocabulary with students, the teacher reads the selection aloud to the class. Next, SLIFE read the selection on their own. Once students have had a chance to review the selection, they take turns reading different sentences aloud; more proficient SLIFE read paragraphs from the selection. Afterwards they work in pairs, taking turns reading sentences or paragraphs aloud to each other and correcting each other's mistakes in pronunciation.

This is followed by retelling the story using "story organization" markers—a rope, several strands of yarn, or any thick piece of material with knots. Each knot represents a different aspect of organization, for example, the introduction, events, and conclusion. Some teachers add strings or branches to include reminders of key characters or related events. Each student stands in front of the class or a small group and retells the story, holding and touching the knots of the story organization marker to remember the different parts of the story.

For SLIFE, such a visual and tactile guide is often very useful to help them remember story organization and development. By touching or even just looking at this memory marker, students can tap into ways of remembering that may be more salient than the printed word or pictures. This activity is not limited to the retelling of fiction but can also be used to help present and review such content as historical events and scientific information.

One memory marker we have seen used with SLIFE is the "story grammar marker" offered by Mind Wing Concepts, Inc.

Resource Tip

An image of the story grammar marker developed by Mind Wing Concepts, Inc., is available at http://mindwingconcepts.com.

The story grammar marker serves as a tool to help students remember the key elements of a story they tell and then write down, or vice versa. The key elements represented by different areas on this marker are:

- character
- setting
- initiating event (kick-off)
- internal response (emotion or feelings)
- plan
- attempts
- direct consequence(s)
- resolution

As story tellers recount a story, they move their fingers from one part of the marker to the next.

It should be noted that one instructor who used the story grammar marker with high school students related that while her female SLIFE and male students from Africa were comfortable holding and using the marker in front of the class, her male Hispanic SLIFE were resistant to using it because they felt it looked too much like a doll. For teachers who encounter such resistance, one possible solution is to encourage reluctant SLIFE to design their own story grammar markers. Developing their own mnemonic tool encourages students to take responsibility for their own earning.

Expansion

After students have read, discussed, and retold a given reading selection, they will write a few paragraphs summarizing the text. The length of the summary will depend on student proficiency level. SLIFE then exchange their paragraphs with a peer and make comments on each other's papers, using a peer conference guide to help them focus their questions. The teacher circulates among the conference pairs to offer help, and feedback and to ensure that students stay on task. Students consider peer comments in the process of rewriting their paragraph and bring the revised version to class the following day. An example form is shown.

SAMPLE PEER CONFERENCE FORM

1. I like the paragraph because _____
   _____.

2. The best thing about the paragraph is _____
   _____.

3. The author needs to add details to_____
   _____.

4. I didn't understand _____.

5. The author misspelled these words: _____.

Resource Tip

Dixon, C., & Nixon, D. (1983). *Language experience approach to reading (and writing): Language experience reading for second language learners.* Hayward, CA: Alemany Press.

We have found that many teachers successfully use the Language Experience Approach with SLIFE. The activity begins by establishing a context, such as listening to a story, watching a movie, or going on a field trip. The teacher then reads his or her own story, reflection, or account based on the shared experience to the class and checks afterwards to be sure students understood the reading. Next, students describe the shared experience in their own words as the teacher writes their sentences on the board or a flipchart. (The teacher provides appropriate help during this process.) Students copy "their" story into their notebooks and this story becomes the basis for a variety of reading and writing, and follow-up activities developed by the teacher.

Wh- Question Practice

SLIFE enjoy participating in this "game," becoming very involved and adept at giving hints, catching each other's mistakes, and making corrections.

With everyone standing or sitting in a circle, the teacher or a designated student starts out by making a statement, and then asks a question. The student to the right of the "questioner" responds. All responses and subsequent questions must be in the form of complete sentences. For example, Student A says to Student B, "My name is Kebe. What's your name?" Student B responds, "My name is Hajera." Hajera then turns to Student C and asks, "What's your name?"

If students respond by simply stating their names, they are out of the "game"; they must stand up if the rest of the group is sitting down, or sit down if everyone is standing. Questions such as "What's yours?" or "What your name is?" or "What your name?" are also unacceptable responses. This game can also be used for SLIFE to review content, using questions such as "Where did the Pilgrims land?" or "When did Columbus come to the New World?"

The questions and content can be very basic for low-proficiency SLIFE. For these students, the teacher may initially want to provide question patterns and key vocabulary on the board to help them ask and answer questions.

SAMPLE QUESTION PATTERNS
• Where is / was
• Where did
• When did
• Who is / was

Expansion

For more proficient SLIFE, the sentences and anticipated answers used in the *wh*-game can be varied in terms of complexity and discipline content. For science review, students can ask questions such as "What is fauna?" or "Why do snakes hibernate in winter?" For a history review, students can ask such questions as "Where was the Magna Carta signed?" or "What right is guaranteed by the Second Amendment of the U.S. Constitution?" For math, students can ask questions such as "What is a quadratic equation?" or "What is πr^2?"

To help students ask appropriate content questions, the teacher can provide a list of topics (e.g., snakes/hibernation) and/or sentence frames (see page 75). As SLIFE become more proficient, the teacher will want to be sure that this question-answer activity includes questions from the upper levels of Bloom's Taxonomy (see Chapter 5.). Games/exercises of this sort help students make the transition to written English and the critical-thinking skills required of academic English in an active and engaging way.

Sentence Frames

In Chapter 4, we presented a few examples of sentence frames in conjunction with newspaper work in after-school and Saturday programs. Sentence frames are a valuable scaffolding tool in helping SLIFE develop writing skills and the ability to use content vocabulary in complete sentences. Sentence frames can be viewed as templates that allow students to focus on appropriate vocabulary words and phrases without worrying about their inability to generate (correct) sentences.

SAMPLE SENTENCE FRAMES: SCIENCE

1. Think about what you want your students to learn.
2. Come up with sentences that cover main points and include key vocabulary.
3. Take out the words and phrases that you want students to discover.
4. The sentence frames below are general guides. You will want to provide your students with more information—for example, A cell is shaped like _____ ; Reptiles live _____.

- It looks like _____.
- It is shaped like _____.
- _____ is / are like _____ because_____.
- _____ is / are similar to _____.
- _____ is / are different from _____ because_____.
- _____ live _____.

Teachers can provide these sentence frames and ask students to provide oral responses first and then write them later.

Mobile Hangers

A mobile hanger is a simple yet valuable technique for helping SLIFE organize important ideas, themes, events, and facts. The hangers can include any shapes that may help students remember. A very basic mobile hanger can be used to remind students of the names of the central character(s) in a story, with some brief notes about other characters on either side, as shown in the figures on page 76.

Cooperative Learning: Example from Science

In the previous chapter, we discussed the importance of collaborative, small-group learning. The following is an illustration of a popular activity we have seen used successfully with high school SLIFE to help them with lab work in their science classes. The same basic format was used throughout the school year, so SLIFE became accustomed to the routine and were able to focus on the content requirements of each individual assignment.

FIGURE 7: Example of Mobile Hanger

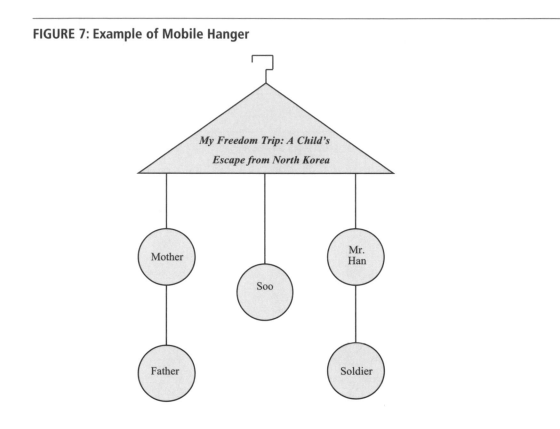

FIGURE 8: Example of Mobile Hanger

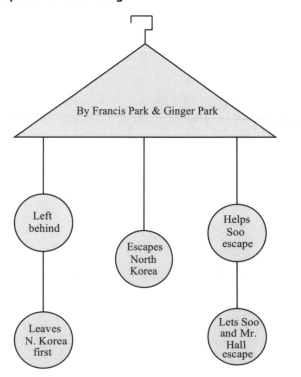

Procedures:

- Each student writes a possible question related to the topic of the experiment on a separate sheet of paper; then, using their individual questions and working together in groups, they collectively come up with one question for the experiment. One person acts as a recorder for the group's final question.

- Each student writes a possible hypothesis on a separate sheet of paper. Using their individual hypotheses as a basis, the group works together to come up with one hypothesis for the experiment. A different person acts as a recorder for the group's final hypothesis.

- Each student suggests one, two, or three items needed for the experiment (the number will differ depending on the nature of a given experiment). A third person acts as a recorder making one list of everyone's suggestions.

- As students work in their groups, the teacher circulates among them to provide individual help and to check that all students remain task focused.

Upon completion of the worksheet, SLIFE interact, helping one another with understanding and reviewing the material, as well as with spelling, vocabulary, and sentence structure.

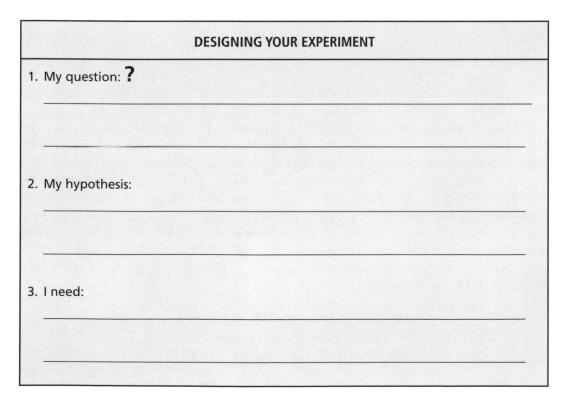

Structural Adaptation of Texts

There are numerous grammatical structures that cause difficulty for SLIFE. Table 3 (page 79) provides a summary of some of the more difficult areas with authentic examples drawn from a popular high school European History textbook.

Field Trips

While we have mentioned the value of field trips in detail elsewhere (see Chapter 5), here we would like to emphasize how important these experiences can be for SLIFE as high-context learners still developing their academic worldview. Field trips, which can range from a discovery walk around the school to longer overnight experiences, provide for multi-contextual experiential learning at its best. Carefully planned and executed field trips

- allow for differentiated learning,
- address multiple intelligences,
- include development of different language skills,
- advance content-area knowledge, and
- develop cognitive thinking skills by focusing on the higher levels of Bloom's Taxonomy (see Chapter 5).

An effective field trip is one that not only exposes SLIFE to something outside of the school environment but provides students with a meaningful context for learning. Students can research and write about topics related to their destinations, and they can take photos or videos during the trip, all of which they can use later to write narratives, develop presentations (including PowerPoint), and Internet-based projects. The combination of visual, oral, tactile, kinesthetic, reading, and written components gives SLIFE rich opportunities to learn new concepts and to revisit and expand on content knowledge in a variety of ways while developing cognitive skills. Field trips help SLIFE develop language, literacy, art, technological, social, and communicative skills. The planning and subsequent follow-up of varied activities—whether journal writing, project development, or completion of graphic organizers—provide SLIFE with a structure and focus for each trip.

> Before I come here, I never think I can read, write good, go to school and learn so many things. I want go college, I want become so many things, I'm so happy in school.
>
> —Ana

> My family, nobody go to school very much, and my mother no school, but I do and I want learn more and more. Is hard for me, I have work very hard, but I know I can do it now.
>
> —Malik

TABLE 3: Grammatical Structures to Watch Out For[1]

Structure	Examples
Pronouns	This last promise had its counterpart throughout all the German states as governments allowed elections by universal male suffrage for deputies to an all-German parliament to meet in Frankfurt, the seat of the German confederations. *Its* purpose was to fulfill a liberal and nationalist dream (p. 597).
Adverbial Clauses	The committee also attempted to provide some economic controls, *especially since members of the more radical working class were advocating them* (p. 540).
	The government could hardly expect peasants to follow the new calendar *when government officials were ignoring it* (p. 541).
	By 1800, most Canadians favored more autonomy, *although the colonists disagreed on the form this autonomy **should** take* (p. 629).
Relative (Adjective) Clauses	The result was a division between the moderate republicans, *who had the support of most of France,* and the radical republican, *whose main support came from the Parisian working class* (p. 596).
Noun Clauses	Darwin was important in explaining *how this natural process worked* (p. 634).
	Some people fretted *that Darwin's theory made human beings ordinary products of nature rather than unique beings* (p. 634).
Phrasal Verbs (also known as two-word verbs)	The king of the northern Italian state of Piedmont, Charles Albert (1931–1849), *took up* the call and assumed the leadership for a war of liberation from Austrian domination.
	Great Britain also *fell behind* in the new chemical industry (p. 643).
Passive Voice	In the elections for the presidency held in December 1848, four republicans who *had been associated* with the early months of the Second Republic *were* resoundingly *defeated* by Charles Louis Napoleon Bonaparte, the nephew of Napoleon Bonaparte (p. 597).
It **(as a "filler" verb)**	*It* is significant, however, that very few of the important discoveries of the eighteenth century occurred in the universities (p. 482).
	It was not until the explorations of Australia by Captain James Cook between 1768 and 1771 that Britain took an active interest in the East (p. 695).

[1] See DeCapua, A., *Grammar for Teachers: A Guide to American English for Native and Non-Native Speakers* (2008b) for more elaboration and examples.

(All examples taken from Spielvogel, J. (2003). *Western Civilization.* (5th ed.). Belmont, CA: Wadsworth/ Thomson Learning.)

Throughout this handbook, we have repeatedly stressed that many of the needs of SLIFE are similar to those of all ELLs. SLIFE, however, need more of everything: more time and patience from teachers; greater focus on literacy skills, background content-area knowledge, and affective factors; and more emphasis on developing cognitive thinking skills and academic worldviews. Though SLIFE require more, this does not mean that successful SLIFE teachers "dumb down" or "water down" their lessons, but it does mean that they utilize a variety of approaches, practices, and techniques to meet the myriad needs of SLIFE and engage and motivate them in school learning. A useful mnemonic for summarizing some of the basic principles for working with SLIFE is SPRAT CRAVES RIBS:

SIMPLE TENSES

PRESERVE MEANING

REDUCE AMOUNT OF MATERIAL

ACTIVE PARTICIPATION VIA SMALL GROUPS

TOPIC SENTENCE FIRST

COLLABORATION

RECYCLE CONCEPTS

AVOID INDEFINITE WORDS

VISUAL AIDS

EMPHASIZE SCAFFOLDING

SENSORY MODES

REPETITION

INTEGRATION OF ALL LANGUAGE SKILLS

BASIC WORD ORDER

SIMPLIFY LANGUAGE, NOT COGNITIVE REQUIREMENTS

The practices, suggestions, and examples presented in this chapter and throughout this book are the result of our classroom observations over several years. This is a handbook, not a piece of scholarly research. As researchers and scholars undertake in-depth studies of SLIFE and their learning styles, we will, without doubt, begin to get a clearer idea of the techniques and strategies that produce the most efficient results within the limited amount of time allocated to high school SLIFE. Obviously, these efforts will require the accumulation of data gathered from a broad range of sources over an extended period of time. In the meantime, we have found it useful to attend national and regional conferences, as well as local workshops and seminars, that focus on SLIFE. Doing so provides teachers/administrators working with this student population opportunities to meet with their counterparts from other schools and to share concerns and practices that have worked with their particular group(s) of students. Establishing avenues of communication and the exchange of ideas among educators at schools, whether on a district, state, or national level, will help all concerned to better serve SLIFE.

Resource Tip

The websites of these two professional organizations provide the dates of national, regional, and local conferences:

- TESOL (Teachers of English to Speakers of Other Languages) www.tesol.org/s_tesol/index.asp
- NABE (National Association of Bilingual Educators) www.nabe.org

Chapter 7

Key Elements of Successful SLIFE Programs

CHAPTER 3 DISCUSSED THE IMPORTANCE OF EDUCATING THE WHOLE CHILD. THIS CHAPTER discusses how educating the whole child means involving the entire school community and families of SLIFE—in keeping with their high-context, collectivistic orientations—in this process. The school community plays an important role in providing SLIFE with structural support, role models, and positive education experiences that promote learning and validate students' identities (Gibson, 2000). Negative attitudes on the part of administrators, support personnel, and/or teachers are barriers to the academic and linguistic success of these students (Nieto, 1991; Freeman & Freeman, 2003; Valdes, 2001), while positive support and positive attitudes toward SLIFE are the cornerstones of successful programs. For many SLIFE, a supportive and fostering school community becomes their second family.

Many SLIFE come from single-parent families or families in which both parents have to work, leaving students frequently without adult supervision or direction to provide frameworks for responsible or socially acceptable behaviors. Due to high housing costs, families of many SLIFE live together with two or three other family groups—often not related—in a space designed to accommodate a single family of three or four people. As a result, students spend as much time as possible outside of the home environment to avoid the overcrowded living conditions and the accompanying stress that could even lead to violence. In our experience, SLIFE could be often found at the school waiting for it to open—the school had become a refuge for them.

For SLIFE, the school may be the only structured environment in their lives, providing many new learning opportunities that most teachers take for granted. Students learn, for example, that time counts; the expectation that SLIFE take responsibility for arriving on time for the start of school and classes leads to more positive learning experiences for SLIFE and prepares them for similar demands of the job market. Second, learning to take responsibility for one's actions and learning to respect oneself—as a person and as a student, with demonstrable academic achievements and accomplishments—emphasizes each student's worth as an individual. Along these lines, the school work of SLIFE, like that of other students, should be prominently displayed in public areas of the school for everyone to see, such as in display cases near building entrances, bulletin boards outside classrooms, in the lunchroom, and so on.

Administrative Support

The support of the entire school community, including principals, guidance counselors, parent coordinators, curriculum supervisors, and other administrators, is vital to the success of any program (Boscardin, 2005). Administrators, by promoting collegial and collaborative learning environments, create supportive school communities that encourage improved educational outcomes for students and more effective instructional practices of teachers (Ruiz-de-Velasco & Fix, 2000). Effective, accountable administrators need to be engaged in these specific practices:

SUCCESSFUL ADMINISTRATIVE SUPPORT
• Careful program planning and implementation in advance of the school year
• Well thought-out decisions regarding which approaches and practices will be used
• Acquisition, allocation, and monitoring of necessary resources
• Hiring of trained support staff, ideally bilingual speakers familiar with the cultures of the students
• On-going communication among administrative personnel, ESL teachers, content-area teachers and support staff
• Establishing and maintaining communication with parents/guardians of SLIFE
• Supporting and arranging for on-going professional development for teachers of SLIFE
• Arranging and accommodating the special scheduling needs of SLIFE
• The allocation of classroom space
• Assessment of the impact of implemented program elements

In planning and/or assessing a SLIFE program and involvement of appropriate personnel, a checklist like this one is helpful to ensure that everyone necessary to the success of the program is included.

Name	Nature of Involvement	Type of License or Certificate
1)	Coordinator	ESL
2)	Teacher	ESL
3)	Teacher/Researcher	Special Ed
4)	Collaborating Content Teacher	Social Studies
5)	Collaborating Content Teacher	Math
6)	Social Work Counseling Support	Bilingual Social Worker
7)	Parent Engagement	Parent Coordinator
8)	Supervisor	Supervisor/Administrator

The Principal

School principals are essential to the success of programs for SLIFE; as leaders, they shape the school community and influence the promotion of collegial and collaborative learning environments (Garcia, 1991). To facilitate the effectiveness of programs for SLIFE in their schools, principals must have first-hand knowledge of the unique needs of this student population, and they must actively support and promote on a daily basis the efforts of school personnel who work with these students.

> Our principal is great. What we need, she gets for us.
> She understands these students; she understands what
> we're working with and what we're trying to do. She's always
> there for us.
>
> —Joy, HS teacher

Supportive principals hold weekly meetings with faculty and make sure that everyone is focused on those SLIFE who need particular attention, whether academic, emotional, or disciplinary. They are in the halls with the students between class changes, in the lunchroom, and in the recreation area—not necessarily to act as overseers but to take advantage of opportunities to talk and interact with the students under these less-structured circumstances. Supportive principals learn the names of as many SLIFE as possible. It is important for principals, as well as teachers and support personnel, to communicate personally with SLIFE, so they are, as one principal stated, "in the loop all the time."

Devoted and Well-Trained Teachers

> These students are really special, really needy. It takes
> so much time, so much patience, sometimes you wonder if
> it's worth it, but when they finally get it and you see their
> excitement, or they come back to you later and show you
> what they can do, then you *know* it's worth it.
>
> —Mary Ellen, HS teacher

A large part of student success is linked to effective teachers who, among other characteristics, exhibit great dedication to and empathy with their students (Antrop-Gonzalez, 2005; Garcia, 1997). In teaching second languages, according to Nunan (1991), "Perhaps the most important article of faith is that the learner's emotional attitude towards the teacher, towards fellow learners, and towards the target language and culture, is the single most important variable in language learning. It is crucial, not only to take account of this factor, but to give it a central place in the selection of content, materials and learning activities" (p. 236).

AN EYEWITNESS STORY

One late afternoon, almost near the end of the after-school SLIFE program one of the authors was observing, a teacher rushed in with plates of cookies for the students. She had been marking test papers in the school district head office and had been excused from teaching in the after-school SLIFE program on that day. Yet she came to school anyway, saying "I saw all the cookies left at the district. So I just grabbed them and brought them back for the kids."

A few plates of cookies may not be worth much, but it is the spirit of caring and loving in that gesture that matters. When the teacher went out of her way to bring the cookies back to school for the SLIFE in the after-school program, she did much more than her role as a teacher required. Watching as the kids munched on the cookies and continued with their work, she said to the author with a big smile, "Who wouldn't do this for these kids?"

—MKB

Seizing opportunities, such as the availability of leftover cookies, to share an experience with students may not seem terribly important or necessary to their learning process. But small gestures of this sort let the students know that the teacher is thinking of them—even outside of school and the classroom. These demonstrations of thoughtfulness are particularly important for ELLs and SLIFE who often feel they have been uprooted and placed in what they may perceive as an unfriendly or even hostile environment. They go a long way toward making SLIFE feel a part of a valued relationship, which is essential to members of collectivistic cultures.

There is no doubt that the dedication and commitment of the teachers who work with SLIFE and who provide the extra time, attention, patience, and caring that they require are critical to the success of these students. Beyond the requisite demands of professional training, these teachers must, above all, be sincerely concerned about and care deeply for this segment of the student population. They must be prepared to try and meet the many needs, ranging from academic to emotional to physical, that SLIFE bring to the classroom and the school. Although they are not counselors, teachers represent for these high-context, collectivistic students, persons with whom they have special relationships and who provide a bridge between home and school. Strong, positive bonds between students and teachers play a significant role in student achievement (Nieto, 2000; Valenzuela, 1999).

> My teacher treats me like big sister, helping me, giving me attention all time. I don't feel hesitating to share anything, joys and worries both with my teacher.
>
> —Xiu, SLIFE

In addition to caring deeply for their students, teachers of SLIFE should

- understand the needs of SLIFE and search for their interests.
- become familiar with their culture, their home country, the geography and basic history of the areas from which their SLIFE come.
- be thoroughly trained in ESL approaches and practices.
- have literacy training because many SLIFE have only basic literacy skills.
- regularly update their professional skills and knowledge by taking part in learning opportunities relevant to their work.
- be flexible, creative, and patient.
- have clear but high expectations for their students.
- work closely with content-area teachers of SLIFE.
- actively encourage open communication with school administration and SLIFE parents/guardians.

Resource Tip

The Center for Applied Linguistics (CAL) offers extensive professional development and professional development materials based on its successful SIOP model:

www.cal.org/siop/index.html

The Classroom

Research supporting the view that the classroom's physical set-up greatly influences how conducive it is to student learning has been around for many decades (e.g., Boocock, 1966; Cooper, 1944; Enright & McCloseky, 1985; Hilligoss, 1992; Leavitt, 1959; Maslinoff, 1969; Papalia, 1976). Nevertheless, a surprisingly large number of classrooms still consists of the traditional arrangement with students sitting in straight rows of desks. Such traditional configurations perpetuate teacher-centered, whole-class instruction; offer few opportunities for group and peer learning experiences or the development of student learning communities; and generally limit students' active engagement in learning (Au & Mason, 1981; Faltis, 2006; Peregoy & Boyle, 2008; Ramírez & Merino, 1990).

To encourage maximum participation and learning among SLIFE, less traditional classroom configurations should be considered. Teachers should view their classrooms as composed of several different learning spaces, with possibilities for multiple uses. One teacher we observed chose to separate her SLIFE classroom into mini-classrooms by using moveable blackboards as space dividers. This allowed for different groups to engage in various targeted learning activities under her direction and the assistance of an aide. During a given period, one group might work on math skills, another on basic literacy, and yet another on social studies. The moveable blackboards permitted the teacher to change the classroom configuration easily in order to accommodate changing student needs. These blackboards provided a sense of separate learning spaces, so the various groups could remain focused and on task; however, because no group was completely distinct or separate from the others, their sense of community remained intact.

Student desks in this classroom were grouped facing each other, rather than the front of the room. The teacher sat at a student desk with SLIFE as a member of the group with which she was currently working. Learning was active and participatory; the role of the teacher was that of a facilitator.

A computer station, reading area, and a small library with books appropriate to SLIFE reading and English proficiency levels were available to students throughout the day, including lunch and any free periods. These resources were arranged around the perimeter of the classroom in less trafficked areas, so SLIFE could use them even when regular class groups were being conducted.

At times, ESL teachers of SLIFE, in particular those who may service more than one school in a district, may find themselves without their own classroom due to lack of space or overcrowding. In such cases, itinerant teachers need to "make do" negotiating with their more anchored colleagues for some space they can use for the benefit of SLIFE. In order to maximize the potential of a less-than-ideal space, teachers will want to think creatively about how to make the most of the space they have. Teachers may want to make a floor plan of their allotted space and consider how it can be functionally arranged to best encourage and support SLIFE, keeping in mind the variety of student needs, abilities, and learning styles.

A Well-Planned Program

Because many factors may have a potential impact on the success programs for SLIFE, it is critical that these programs be carefully planned well in advance of their implementation—no matter how pressing the need to put such a program in place.

QUESTIONS TO CONSIDER BEFORE ESTABLISHING A PROGRAM FOR SLIFE
• What school policies need to be changed?   • What programs need to be put into place?   • What special training and/or professional development support will they require?

Planners should keep in mind that a poorly planned and executed program for SLIFE is of little or no more use than no program at all. Good planning requires knowledge of what is needed and where to find it. When putting together a team to work with SLIFE, clear-cut goals and objectives that address the needs of specific SLIFE must be established. Team members must be familiar with the resources available to them within the school and district, in addition to other potential sources of support, including

- community- and religious-based service organizations
- private businesses and corporations that assist public schools
- non-profit foundations
- institutes of higher education (colleges and universities) that may be willing to partner or assist with the program

Because different approaches have different underlying assumptions about the nature of language, learning, and teaching, and consequently engender various preferred classroom practices (Anthony, 1963; Richards & Rogers, 2001), the SLIFE team must also carefully evaluate and choose which approach and practices will best suit their student population (see Chapter 5) and fit into the larger school community. The decision to use a particular approach will serve as a guide for

- planning assessment strategies for SLIFE
- determining the nature of other activities built into the program to help SLIFE compensate for their "lost" education time
- facilitating the transition of SLIFE into mainstream classes and ensuring their success

Adoption of a particular approach usually means that at least one member of the team receives training by experts in the use of effective ESL practices and/or literacy strategies. This individual then becomes the "turnkey" or designated instructor responsible for training the other members of the team in the effective use of these practices and strategies. Not all schools can or should employ the same approach for working with SLIFE; yet, those that can be designated as schools with "best practices" for SLIFE have chosen one particular approach that serves as a structural framework for their programs while at the same time allowing for flexibility among the teaching staff to meet the needs of individual SLIFE. And while different schools across the U.S. may use the same approach, there is significant flexibility in the way(s) each school actually implements it.

Sharing a common approach and practices does not mean that teachers need adhere to every tenet, but it does mean that there is a framework within which to work without interfering with creative practices necessary to achieve the goals established for SLIFE. Effective programs allow for the greatest flexibility on the part of teachers and SLIFE, given the constraints of scheduling and curriculum at their schools. Effective programs also continually assess themselves. When something is not working with SLIFE, teachers need to find out what needs to be changed and how to implement the change. Being able to adapt to the needs of a particular group of students and having the support of the school administration for such flexibility is vital to a successful program. A consensus on one approach ensures that changes are based on a common understanding of the direction and execution of the overall program for SLIFE.

Team Teaching

Team teaching is an important component of a successful SLIFE program. Extensive cooperation among content teachers and ESL teachers makes for more effective learning. Schools that have made a sincere commitment to team teaching have built blocks of time into the schedules of content and ESL teachers to coordinate and plan lessons. There must be a common preparation time for all teachers involved in order for this to work.

Part of the team planning process involves identifying the most important aspects of each lesson, keeping in mind that what may seem obvious to teachers may not be so for SLIFE. All lessons must not only teach content and promote English and literacy skills but also develop students' academic worldviews or formal learning paradigms (DeCapua & Marshall, forthcoming; Flynn, 2007). Because each content area has its own discourse and organizational styles, team teaching encourages ESL and content-area teachers to work together, each in his or her area of expertise, on how to adapt content materials without watering them down.

Articulation

Successful teaching practices involve articulation. Given the number of people involved directly and indirectly with SLIFE (e.g., teachers, principals, assistant principals, scheduling personnel, guidance counselors, parent coordinators, and social workers), strong leadership is required. Designated teams, composed of those who are directly responsible for the success of SLIFE programs, should meet regularly to share experiences and impressions and review program goals. Team members should address a range of topics to ensure that students are being exposed to the best possible learning opportunities.

ARTICULATION TOPICS

- Review of each individual student's progress in all subject areas
- Discussion of students' particular strengths that need encouragement
- Examination of areas where extra work is called for in order to bring the students up to their set levels of achievement
- Consideration of any academic, emotional, physical, and/or other issues that need follow-up with school counselors, the school nurse, other support staff, and/or parents, if necessary
- Review of whether there is a system in place to provide support for any necessary interventions, whether physical, emotional, family, or social

---

Program Assessment and Improvement

Ongoing program assessment must be conducted by team members to assure that the quality of the programs offered for SLIFE is meeting students' needs. The questions listed should be asked regularly.

QUESTIONS TO CONSIDER WHEN ASSESSING A PROGRAM

1. Consider each and every SLIFE.
   - Is the student learning? How can this be demonstrated? For example, what progress do you see in a student's writing?
   - What changes do you see in a student's reading abilities, specifically in
     - decoding skills?
     - fluency reading?
   - What changes have you seen in class participation?
     - Is a student becoming more active in whole-class activities? In small-group work?
   - What approach/techniques have been successful with the student?
     - How do you know this?
   - How might the program change to better meet the needs of the student?
   - What additional resources and/or training are needed to better help the student?
2. How are goals modified if the needs of SLIFE are not being adequately met?
3. Are there realistic and well-planned exit strategies for SLIFE as part of the program profile? How can this be demonstrated?
4. Has the student population changed since the program for SLIFE was implemented?
   - If yes, are the needs of the new students different? How so?

The check sheet on page 91 can be used to summarize key aspects of the SLIFE program to assist team members when assessing the program.

SLIFE Program Objectives, Activities, and Evaluation

Objectives:

Activities:

Quantitative Assessment Instruments:

Qualitative Assessment Techniques:

Exit Strategies

Carefully planned exit strategies for SLIFE are critical to a successful program and should be determined on an individual basis with input from the SLIFE team. The exit strategies must be the product of a group effort that includes:

- the ESL instructor
- content area teachers
- the guidance counselor
- parent coordinator(s)
- others who have spent significant time working with SLIFE, such as aides, the school librarian, or the school psychologist

Preliminary exit plans can be drawn up based on the student's age, skills at time of enrollment, and projected realistic goals. These plans should be revised after the members of the team have had time to become familiar with the student and can then make better-informed decisions.

Rigid exit deadlines are not realistic for SLIFE, given the myriad of challenges they face. Exit times must be flexible and reflect the specific needs of each student and his or her goals and plans. Decisions regarding the exit of a student from a SLIFE program should not be based solely on standardized tests, which are not likely to be appropriate for or provide an accurate and reliable picture of ELLs in general (Abedi, Hofstetter, & Lord, 2004; Faltis & Coulter, 2008; Ovando, Collier, & Combs, 2003), let alone SLIFE. Evaluation of a student's preparedness to move into ESL or mainstream programs should include other measurable evidence of academic performance, such as a student's class and homework assignments, oral and written reports, worksheets, lab projects, PowerPoint presentations, and portfolios.

Portfolios

Portfolios are a particularly valuable way of assessing student performance and progress over time. Students, in consultation with their teachers, collect representative samples of their work in all classes. Because portfolios are collections of student work, they provide a picture of student growth and development rather than a one-shot view. Portfolio assessments help motivate students and encourage increased student involvement in the learning process because they take responsibility for selecting representative work and recognizing what they have accomplished, as well as recognizing which areas need more work (Brown & Hudson, 1998; Genessee & Upshur, 1996). Good portfolios include not only examples of students' best work but also provide evidence of their learning process (e.g., multiple drafts of a piece of writing, different stages of a project).

In some schools, we have seen assessments of mid-year and final portfolios of SLIFE that also include an oral component. For each content area, students present representative samples from their portfolios and explain essential concepts that they have learned to at least two teachers. Students are graded on their portfolios overall and on their oral presentations.

The portfolios and presentations are generally assessed based on rubrics developed by the SLIFE team. The difficulties many teams face in developing an appropriate rubric is setting accurate standards that are transparent to those who will be using the rubric and that will produce reliable assessments among all the raters (Arter & Spandel, 1992).

Meaningful, Standards-Based Learning

> These kids may not have a lot of academic experience, but their life experiences are well beyond their grade and age levels.
>
> —Belinda, HS SLIFE Teacher

In the preparation, presentation, and assessment of their lessons, teachers must work within the parameters of standards mandated by the state within which SLIFE are being educated and in accordance with NCLB. In the case of SLIFE, mandated standards are likely to be well beyond students' initial capabilities; however, this does not mean that these standards should be abandoned altogether. Teachers need to explore different ways of adapting lessons to make them meaningful and accessible to SLIFE, while incorporating the objectives set forth in state standards.

In successful classes of SLIFE, teachers develop lessons that are standards based yet accommodate the different proficiency and ability levels within each class. Students are regularly assessed to determine if they have met the mandated standards; depending on the results, SLIFE move to the next academic and/or proficiency level or work with teachers and/or peer tutors to review specific material and learning strategies that will support their advancement.

When adapting standards-based curriculum to meet the language needs of SLIFE, the content and nature of the materials used in the lessons should be age appropriate. Just because a seventeen-year-old student may read on a second grade level does not mean that this learner should automatically be given second grade children's books. While some children's books may be relevant and useful to older students (see Chapter 2), many are not appropriate in terms of content; they can also be difficult in their own way, often characterized by the use of different verb tenses and the frequent use of phrasal verbs, colloquialisms, and idioms.

Although it requires additional effort, teachers can adapt grade-level texts and materials to a variety of different ability levels (see Chapter 6), keeping in mind that adaptation is not the same as "dumbing down" lessons, which does a great disservice to SLIFE. Studies have shown that there is a tendency among mainstream teachers with ELLs to water or "dumb" down lessons (Gersten & Woodward, 1994; Ramirez, 1992). Teachers of SLIFE need to adapt language and content for their students, without lessening their expectations of them. Low English proficiency and lack of content knowledge are not indicators of academic ability or potential. Providing greater con-textualization of academic material supports all learners and does not reflect lower expectations or the need for remediation. Good teaching encompasses high expecta-tions for one's students, resulting in more successful learning (Garcia, 1997).

A School Community

ELLs are often made to feel as though they are outsiders rather than part of the total school community (Kozol, 2005; Olsen & Jaramillo, 1999). This is even truer for SLIFE who, because of affective, academic, and literacy issues, frequently feel even less a part of the larger school community. As humanistic principles of teaching sug-gest (see Chapter 3), students who feel that they belong and that they are valued are more likely to be successful academically (Gibson, Gándara, & Koyama, 2004). In order to experience a sense of academic participation and achievement, SLIFE need to develop an academic identity, that is, an understanding of self as a mem-ber of a school community that values the pursuit of literacy and academic knowl-edge (Jackson, 2003). The inclusion process should start before the first day of the school year and should involve parents/guardians, so they too feel a part of the school community.

Communication with Parents

High schools are often overwhelming for both SLIFE and their parents/guardians. Let students and parents know that your school community is a welcoming community. Encourage all extended family members of SLIFE to participate in programs and activ-ities. This is especially important for families coming from collectivistic cultures in which the family is regarded as a unified group and social relationships are as impor-tant, if not more so, as academic achievements (Trumball et al., 2001).

The importance of establishing avenues of communication with SLIFE and their families cannot be emphasized enough. Open communication between the school community and parents/guardians is an important part of a successful educational process (Becher, 1984; Delgado-Gaitan, 1991; Walsh, 1999). When parents/guardians are more involved in schools, students have fewer behavior problems, higher achieve-ment, and lower dropout rates (Plevyak & Heaston, 2001). The involvement of prin-cipals, parent coordinators, guidance counselors, and teachers in the communication process often helps parents realize the importance of the efforts being made by the school on behalf of their children, in addition to the role that they play as parents/ guardians. In many SLIFE cultures, teachers and adminstrators are viewed as impor-tant authority figures, not only in the school but in the larger community as well, and their counsel carries a great deal of weight.

Because many SLIFE come from cultures and/or families where oral transmis-sion is the norm, parents/guardians may not understand written notes from teachers, flyer announcements, or similar printed material. Whenever possible, teachers and/

or support personnel should personally contact students' parents/guardians to invite them to school events and on class trips, or to convey important information about their child, the school, or other events. The nature of communication plays a major role in the degree to which parents/guardians feel welcomed and become involved (Hoover-Dempsey & Sandler, 1997). We have found that the most successful communication between parents/guardians and the school occurs when teachers, with the help of interpreters as needed, take an active role in telephoning families of SLIFE and communicating with parents/guardians about their children's school performance and school events. In certain cases, where it has been feasible to do so, teachers have visited families of SLIFE and have been able to establish effective bonds.

Parents/guardians of SLIFE should participate in the plan for their children's graduation, so everyone is clear on the academic requirements for SLIFE and the time frame in which they are expected to meet them. Because parents/guardians themselves often struggle with print, the school should meet with them to discuss the graduation plan, using an interpreter if needed. If face-to-face communication is not feasible, a phone call is recommended. The school also needs to regularly inform parents/guardians of SLIFE, through oral and written communication of their children's progress and/or any problems they may be having.

COMMUNICATING WITH PARENTS/GUARDIANS OF SLIFE TO HELP THEM UNDERSTAND

- why it is important that their children regularly attend specially scheduled classes, especially if SLIFE have after-school or weekend jobs to supplement family income
- the nature and purpose of SLIFE programs
- why their children were selected to take part in these SLIFE programs
- the specific goals for their children
- the benefits of attending programs for SLIFE
- the times specially scheduled programs take place (e.g., before or after the official school day, or on Saturdays)

Orientation Programs

Schools should have a specific SLIFE orientation program just before the school year begins, or as soon as possible after the term has begun, to help all students adjust and to begin the inclusion process for SLIFE. To maximize the value of orientation programs, include student volunteers and parents. They are valuable assets in making school procedures and the general environment more accessible and comprehensible to SLIFE and their parents/guardians.

Orientation programs for SLIFE should include a tour of the school, including classrooms, and other facilities. Such a tour will help open doors to communication and make everyone feel more comfortable with the school, the staff, and the facilities. During orientation programs, students and parents/guardians of SLIFE should also have the opportunity to meet with administrators, teachers, and support staff. Let them know who is who and who does what. Be sure that SLIFE know who their guidance counselors are and how these counselors can help them. Include time to inform SLIFE and their parents/guardians of school and program expectations. Make parents/guardians aware of any programs at your school or in the community that might benefit them.

Parental Involvement

Getting the parents/guardians of SLIFE involved with school programs can be difficult, no matter how concerned they may be about their children's education. There are several reasons for this. Parents/guardians may feel uncomfortable in the school; work long hours, with little or no time available to participate; fear contact with authorities if they have uncertain immigration status; and/or want to avoid confronting a language barrier at school if there is no one available to interpret for them (Ariza, 2002; Olivos & Quintana de Valladolid, 2005). In addition, when families come from cultures where education is the exclusive domain of the teacher and school, parents/guardians may not be comfortable with or aware of U.S. expectations, and indeed their rights, to participate in educational decisions for their children.

Nevertheless, as we and others (e.g., Trumball et al., 2001) have observed, parents/guardians of SLIFE gradually become more involved if they are provided with sufficient opportunities to participate and made to feel that they, too, are valued and appreciated. Asking parents to chaperone SLIFE and/or other students on field trips, for example, is a means of bridging the space between school and home and giving parents/guardians an opportunity to learn more about their new community. How they are invited often plays a major role in how much they become involved—whether a telephone call or a handwritten note—the more personal the invitation, the more likely parents/guardians are to respond positively than they are to general, impersonal form letters or flyers.

Some schools have also encouraged involvement of parents/guardians by providing food, and containers for taking home leftovers, at any gathering that involves them. As one school administrator expressed to us,

> Having those plastic containers, you know the Glad ones or whatever that you can get at the supermarket or Costco for not a lot of money, have made a difference in getting them here. We've tried asking why but nobody seems to know. We just know it works, so we keep doing it. We have food, lots of it, and lots of containers whenever we plan anything—parent-teacher conferences, workshops, anything.
>
> —R.S., School Administrator

Workshops have also proven to be a positive way to involve parents in many of the schools we have observed. Workshops are offered in the native language(s) of the parents or with an interpreter present if the workshop presenter does not speak the native language(s). These workshops cover such topics as the basics of the U.S. high school system, school regulations, tips for helping their children at home with school, basic life skills, issues of citizenship, and computer literacy. Some schools partner with banks to present workshops on savings and checking accounts; others open their weight room for parent/guardian use while SLIFE participate in Saturday programs. Any programs for parents/guardians that bring them into the school and help them feel comfortable with and a part of the school community are invaluable in building school and family relationships.

As emphasized throughout this book, SLIFE need more simply because they have had less: less time in school, less access to quality education in their native countries, and fewer opportunities to discover their academic abilities. While their needs are many, schools have an obligation to find and make available the resources necessary to help SLIFE adapt to their new environment and develop the tools they need to become productive citizens. At the core of this effort are caring, concerned teachers and school administrators who are willing to make the extra effort to plan, organize, implement, and coordinate those elements necessary for the establishment of a successful program for SLIFE.

MARCOS'S STORY

At 14 years old, Marcos was brought to the United States by his parents, who had come to this country several years earlier from a rural area of Mexico. He and his three sisters had been left behind with their grandmother until their parents were able to send for them. Marcos was placed in high school, even though in Mexico he had only completed through third grade. His English skills were limited to only a few phrases and colloquial expressions, such as "Whas' up?"

After a year in the SLIFE program, Marcos has made remarkable strides, due to a combination of his determination to succeed and the support he has received from the school community. He became fascinated by computer technology and devotes hours to preparing PowerPoint presentations, using Adobe PhotoShop, and researching information on the Internet. He is taking both SLIFE English language arts and native language arts. His writing skills have improved significantly, and he hopes someday to become a writer or newspaper reporter so that "I can tell everybody what really happening in world, how other people live, how suffer."

Marcos is never shy about asking for extra help and takes advantage of everything he can to learn: "I like everything, social studies is hard because so many new things, so many vocabulary, but math, science I like. Especially experiments we do."

Appendix: Graphic Organizers

The following are some of the more commonly used graphic organizers we have seen used with SLIFE. These should be modified and adapted to fit the needs of particular students and subject material.

1. Series of Events

Used to show the logical sequence of events.

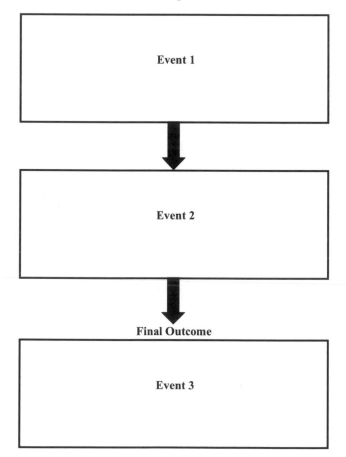

2. Web

Used to show main idea and connecting ideas or main theme and related topics. Can be used to show vocabulary word definitions and/or synonyms.

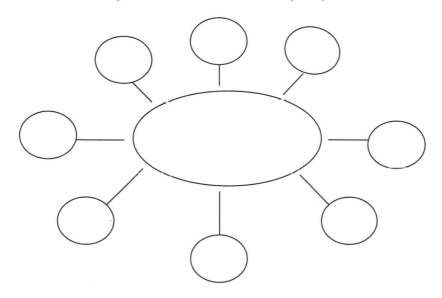

3. Venn Diagram

Used to make comparisons and contrasts. Differences are listed in the outer parts of the circles; similarities in the shared, middle area.

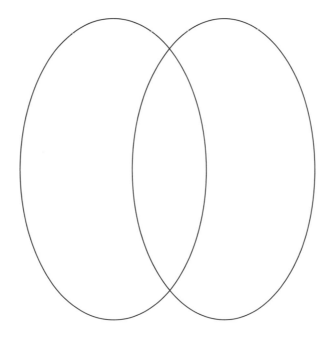

4. Cycle

Used to show chain of repeating events, actions, and occurrences.

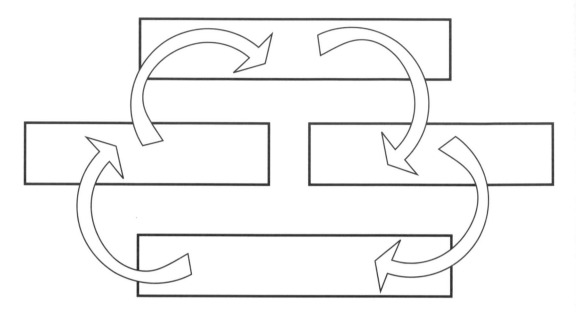

5. Cause & Effect

Used to show how an action, event, or occurrence has specific outcomes.

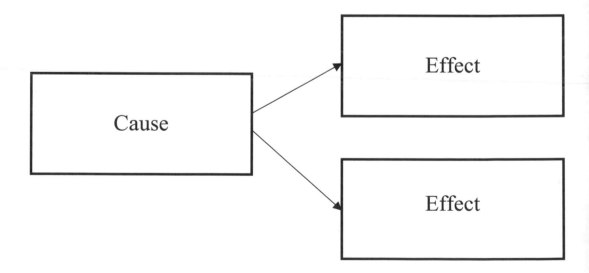

References

Abedi, J., Hofstetter, C., & Lord, C. (2004). Assessment accommodations for English language learners: Implications for policy-based empirical research. *Review of Educational Research, 74,* 1–28.

Akinnaso, N.F. (1992). Schooling, language, and knowledge in literate and nonliterate societies. *Comparative Studies in Society and History, 34,* 68–109.

Antrop-González, R. (2005). ¿Dónde están los estudiantes puertorriqueños exitosos? [Where are the academically successful Puerto Rican students?]: Success factors of high-achieving Puerto Rican high school students. *Journal of Latinos and Education, 4,* 77–94.

Anthony, E. (1963). Approach, method and technique. *English Language Teaching, 17,* 63–67.

Apfel, R., & Simon, B. (Eds.). (1996). *Minefields in their hearts: The mental health of children in war and communal violence.* New Haven, CT: Yale University Press.

Ariza, E. N. (2002). Cultural considerations: Immigrant parent involvement. *Kappa Delta Pi Record, 38,* 134–137.

Arroyo, W., & Eth, S. (1996). Post-traumatic stress disorder and other stress reactions. In R. Apfel & B. Simon, *Minefields in their hearts: The mental health of children in war and communal violence* (pp. 52–74). New Haven, CT: Yale University Press.

Arter, J. A., & Spandel, V. (1992). Using portfolios of student work in instruction and assessment. *Educational Measurement: Issues and Practice, 1,* 36–44.

Artiles, A. J., Trent, S. C., & Palmer, J. D. (2004). Culturally diverse students in special education: Legacies and prospects. In J. Banks & C. A. McGee Banks (Eds.), *Handbook of research on multicultural education* (pp. 716–735). San Francisco: Jossey-Bass.

Asher, J. (1982). *Learning another language through actions: The complete teacher's guidebook.* Los Gatos, CA: Sky Oaks Productions.

Au, K., & Mason, J. (1981). Social organizational factors in learning to read: The balance of rights hypothesis. *Reading Research Quarterly, 17,* 115–152.

August, D., & Shanahan, T. (Eds.). (2006). *Developing reading and writing in second language learners.* Washington, DC: Center for Applied Linguistics. Mahwah, NJ: Lawrence Erlbaum.

Baker, C. (2006). *Foundations of bilingual education and bilingualism.* (4th ed.). Bristol, England: Multilingual Matters.

Barr, R., Sadow, M., and Blachowicz, C. (1990). *Reading diagnosis for teachers: An instructional approach.* New York: Longman.

Barton, P. (2005). *One-third of a nation: Rising dropout rates and declining opportunities.* Princeton, NJ: Educational Testing Services.

Becher, R. M. (1984). *Parent involvement: A review of research and principles of successful practice.* Washington, DC: National Institute of Education.

Bennett, C. (2007). *Comprehensive multicultural education: Theory and practice.* (6th ed.). New York: Pearson.

Bloom B. (1956). *Taxonomy of educational objectives, Handbook I: The cognitive domain.* New York: David McKay.

Boocock, S. (1966). Toward a sociology of learning: A selective review of existing research. *Sociology of Education, 39,* 1–45.

Boscardin, M. L. (2005) The administrative role in transforming secondary schools to support inclusive evidence-based practices. *American Secondary Education Journal, 33,* 21–32.

Boyson, J. & Short, D. (2003). *Secondary school newcomer programs in the United States*. Washington, DC: Center for Applied Linguistics.

Brinton, D., Snow, M.A., Wesche, M. (2003). *Content-based second language instruction*. Ann Arbor: University of Michigan Press.

Brown, C. L. (2004). Reducing the over-referral of culturally and linguistically diverse students (CLD) for language disabilities. *NABE Journal of Research and Practice, 2,* 225–243.

Brown, H. D. (2007). *Teaching by principles: An interactive approach to language pedagogy* (3rd edition). New York: Prentice Hall.

Brown, J. D., & Hudson, T. (1998). Alternatives in language assessment. *TESOL Quarterly, 32,* 653–675.

Calderon, M. (1990). *Cooperative learning for limited English proficient students* (Tech Report No. 3). Baltimore: Johns Hopkins University, Center for Research on Effective Schooling for Disadvantaged Students.

Capps, R., Fix, M., Murray, J., Ost, J., Passel, J., & Hernandez, S. (2005). *The new demography of America's schools: Immigration and the No Child Left Behind Act*. Urban Institute. Retrieved January 9, 2008, from www.urban.org/url.cfm?ID=311230

Cazden, C. (1988). *Classroom discourse*. Portsmouth, NH: Heinemann.

Chang, H. (1990). *Newcomer programs: innovative efforts to meet the challenges of immigrant students*. San Francisco: California Tomorrow.

Constantino, R., & Lavadenz, R. (1993). Newcomer schools: First impressions. *Peabody Journal of Education, 69,* 82–101.

Cooper, D. (1944). Improving the design of the general classroom in the elementary school. *The Elementary School Journal, 44,* 465–471.

Crandall, J., Bernacvhe, C., & Prager, S. (1998). New frontiers in educational policy and program development: The challenge of the underschooled immigrant secondary school student. *Educational Policy, 12,* 719–734.

Cummins, J. (1981) Age on arrival and immigrant second language learning in Canada. A reassessment. *Applied Linguistics, 2,* 132–149.

———. (1984). *Bilingualism and special education: Issues in assessment and pedagogy*. Clevedon, UK: Multilingual Matters.

———. (2000). *Language, power, and pedagogy*. Clevedon, UK: Multilingual Matters.

Dalton, S. (1998). *Pedagogy matters: Standards for effective teaching practice*. Santa Cruz, CA: Center for Research on Education, Diversity & Excellence.

Davidson, N. (1990). *Cooperative Learning in mathematics: A handbook for teachers*. Menlo Park, CA: Addison-Wesley.

DeCapua, A. (2008a). From we and us to they: Cross-cultural sensitivity training among eighth graders: A pilot study. *Teaching and Learning: The Journal of Natural Inquiry, 22,* 108–118.

———. (2008b). *Grammar for teachers: A guide to American English for native and non-native speakers*. New York: Springer.

DeCapua. A., & Marshall, H. (forthcoming). *Limited Formally Schooled English Language Learners in U.S. Classrooms*.

DeCapua, A. , Smathers, W., & Tang, F. (2007). Addressing the challenges and needs of Students with Interrupted Formal Education (SIFE). *Educational Policy & Leadership, 65 (5)*: 40–46.

DeCapua, A., & Wintergerst, A. (2004). *Crossing cultures in the language classroom*. Ann Arbor: University of Michigan Press.

Delgado-Gaitan, C. (1991). Involving parents in the schools: A process of empowerment. *American Journal of Education, 100,* 20–46.

Doherty, R., Hilberg, R., Pinal, A., & Tharp, R. (2003). Five standards and student achievement. *NABE Journal of Research and Practice, 1,* 1–24. Retrieved June 5, 2008, from htpp://www.uc.edu/njrp/pdfs/Doherty.pdf

Duke, K., & Mabbot, A. (2001). An alternative model for novice-level elementary ESL education. *WITESOL Journal, 17,* 11–30.

Echevarria, J., Vogt, M. E., & Short, D. (2008). *Making content comprehensible for English language learners: The SIOP model* (3rd ed.). Boston: Allyn & Bacon.

Ellis, R. (1984). *Classroom second language development: A study of classroom interaction and language acquisition.* Oxford, UK: Pergamon.

Enright. D., & McCloskey, M. (1985). Yes, talking!: Organizing the classroom to promote second language acquisition. *TESOL Quarterly, 19,* 431–453.

Faltis, C., & Coulter, C. (2008). *Teaching English learners and immigrant students in secondary schools.* Upper Saddle River, NJ: Pearson.

Feinberg, R. (2000). Newcomer school: Salvation or segregated oblivion for immigrant students? *Theory into Practice, 39,* 220–227.

Fishman, J., & Monroe, R. (1990, June/July). Post-traumatic stress disorder in Salvadoran students. *Central America in the classroom,* p. 3.

Fletcher, G. (September 2007). Signs of things to come. *T.H.E. Journal, 3,* 26–27.

Flynn, J. (2007). *What is intelligence?* New York: Cambridge University Press.

Freeman, Y., & Freeman, S. (2002). *Closing the achievement gap: How to reach limited-formal-schooling and long-term English learners.* Portsmouth, NH: Heinemann.

Friedlander, M. (1991). *The newcomer program: Helping immigrant students succeed in. U.S. schools.* Washington, DC: National Clearing House for Bilingual Education: Program Information Series.

Fry, E., Kress, J., & Fountoukidis, D. (2004). *The reading teacher's book of lists.* Paramus, NJ: Prentice Hall.

Fry, R. (2005). *The higher drop-out rate of foreign-born teens: The role of schooling abroad.* Washington, DC: PEW Hispanic Center.

Fu, D. (2003). *An island of English: Teaching ESL in Chinatown.* Portsmouth, NH: Heinemann.

Gage, N., & Berliner, D. (1991). *Educational psychology* (5th ed.). Boston: Houghton Mifflin.

Gall, M. (November, 1984). Synthesis of research on teachers' questioning. *Educational Leadership,* 40–47.

Garcia, E. (1991). *Education of linguistically and culturally diverse students: Effective instructional practices.* (Educational Practice Report Number 1.) Santa Cruz, CA, and Washington, DC: National Center for Research on Cultural Diversity and Second Language Learning. (ERIC Document Reproduction Service No. ED 338 099).

———. (1997). Effective instruction for language minority students. In A. Darder, R. Torres, & H. Gutierrez (Eds.), *Latinos and education* (pp. 362–372). New York: Routledge.

Gardner, H. (1983/2003). *Frames of mind. The theory of multiple intelligences.* New York: Basic Books.

Gass, S. (1997). *Input, interaction, and the second language learner.* Mahwah, NJ: Lawrence Erlbaum.

Genessee, F., & Upshur, J. (1996). *Classroom-based evaluation in second language education.* Cambridge, UK: Cambridge University Press.

Gersten, R., & Woodward, J. (1994). The language minority student and special education: Issues, themes and paradoxes. *Exceptional Child, 60,* 310–322.

Gibson, M. (2000). Situational and structural rationales for the school performance of immigrant youth. Three cases. In H. Vermeulen & J. Perlmann (Eds.), *Immigrants, schooling and social mobility: Does culture make a difference?* (pp. 72–102). New York: St. Martin's Press.

Gibson, M., Gándara, P., & Koyama, J. (2004). *School connections: U.S. Mexican youth, peers, and school achievement.* New York: Teachers College Press.

Gomez, K., & Madda, C. (2005). Vocabulary instruction for ELL Latino students in the middle school science classroom. *Voices from the Middle, 13*, 42–47.

González, N., & Amati, C. (1997). Teaching anthropological methods to teachers: The transformation of knowledge. In C. Kottak, J. White, R. Furlow, & P. Rice (Eds.), *The teaching of anthropology: Problems, issues and decisions* (pp. 353–359). MountainView, CA: Mayfield.

Gruber, G. (2008). *Gruber's essential guide to test taking* (2ⁿᵈ ed.). Naperville, IL: Sourcebooks.

Gunning, T. (2003). *Building literacy in the content areas* (2ⁿᵈ ed.). Boston: Allyn & Bacon.

————. (2008). *Creating literacy instruction for all children* (6ᵗʰ ed.). New York: Longman.

Hall, E. (1976) *Beyond culture.* New York: Anchor.

Harris, J. H., & Katz, L. G. (2001). *Young investigators: The project approach in the early years.* New York: Teachers College Press.

Henze, R. C., & Lucas, T. (1993). Shaping instruction to promote the success of language minority students: An analysis of four high school classes. *Peabody Journal of Education, 69*, 54–81.

Hilligoss, T. (1992). Demystifying "classroom chemistry": The role of the interactive learning model author(s). *Sociology, 20*, 12–17.

Hofstede, G., & Hofstede, G. (2005). *Cultures and organizations: Software of the mind* (2ⁿᵈ ed.). New York: McGraw-Hill.

Holt, D. D. (Ed.). (1993). *Cooperative learning: A response to linguistic and cultural diversity.* McHenry, IL and Washington, DC: Delta Systems and Center for Applied Linguistics.

Hones, D., & Cha, C. S. (1999). *Educating new Americans: Immigrant lives and learning.* Mahwah, NJ: Lawrence Erlbaum.

Hoover-Dempsey, K., & Sandler, H. (1997). Why do parents become involved in their children's education? *Review of Educational Research, 67*, 3–42.

Hosp, J., & Mulder, M. (Spring, 2003) English language learners in Utah: Trends and future directions. *The Utah Special Educator*, 8–11.

Hyland, K. (2004). *Disciplinary discourses: Social interactions in academic writing.* Ann Arbor: University of Michigan Press.

Ives, B. (2004). Graphic organizers applied to secondary algebra instruction for students with learning disorders. *Learning Disabilities Research & Practice, 22*, 110–118.

Jackson, B. (April, 2003). Education reform as if student agency mattered: Academic microcultures and student identity. *Phi Delta Kappan, 84*, 579–585.

Johnson, J. (2005). *Why rural matters 2005: The facts about rural education in the 50 states.* Arlington, VA: The Rural School and Community Trust.

Kagan, S. (1989). *Cooperative learning: Resources for teachers.* San Juan Capistrano, CA: Resources for Teachers.

Kandel, W., & Cromartie, J. (2004). *New patterns of Hispanic settlement in rural America.* Washington, DC: Economic Research Service.

Kozol, J. (2005). *Shame of the nation: The restoration of apartheid schooling in America.* New York: Crown.

Kratochvil, M. (August 26, 2001). Urban tactics: Translating for parents means growing up fast. *New York Times* (Science Section). Retrieved January 9, 2008, from http://query.nytimes.com/gst/fullpage.html?res=9E06E5DC1331F935A1575BC0A9679C8B63&sec=&spon=&pagewanted=2

Leavitt, J. (1959). Teacher-pupil relationships. *Review of Educational Research, 29*, 209–217.

Liu, M., & Tang, F. (2008) Brain-based learning in a second language classroom. *Idiom, 38*, (1) 11–13.

Loar, L. (2004). Making tangible gains in parent-child relationships with traumatized refugees. *Intervention, 2*, 210–220.

Long, M. (1996). The role of the linguistic environment in second language acquisition. In W. Ritchie and T. Bhatia (Eds.), *Handbook of second language acquisition* (pp. 413–468). San Diego: Academic Press.

Lysgaard, S. (1955). Adjustment in a foreign society: Norwegian Fulbright grantees visiting the United States. *International Social Science Bulletin, 7*, 45–51.

Mace-Matluck, B.J., Alexander-Kasparik, R., & Queen, R. M. (1998). *Through the golden door: Educational approaches for immigrant adolescents with limited formal schooling.* McHenry, IL: Delta Systems.

Mackey, A. (1999). Input, interaction and second language development. *Studies in Second Language Acquisition, 21*, 557–587.

Marshall, H. W. (1998). A mutually adaptive learning paradigm for Hmong students. *Cultural Circles, 3*, 135–149.

Maslinoff, L. (1969). Identifying classroom boundaries. *Theory into Practice, 8*, 168–172.

Maslow, A. (1943). A theory of human motivation. *Psychological Review, 50*, 370–396. Retrieved June 12, 2008, from http://psychclassics.yorku.ca/Maslow/motivation.htm

May, F. (1998). *Reading as communication: To help children write and read.* Upper Saddle River, NJ: Merrill.

Mehan, H. (1979). "What time is it, Denise?": Asking known information questions in classroom discourse. *Theory into Practice, 28*, 285–294.

Meltzer, J., with Smith, N., & Clark, H. (2002). *Adolescent literacy resources: Linking research and practice.* Providence, RI: Northeast and Islands Regional Educational Laboratory at Brown University.

Moje, E., Collazo, T., Carillo, R., & Marx, R. (2001). "Maestro, What is quality?" Language, literacy, and discourse in project-based science. *Journal of Research in Science Teacher, 38*, 469–498.

Moll, L., Amanti, C., Neff, D., & Gonzalez, N. (1992). Funds of knowledge for teaching: Using a qualitative approach to connect homes and classrooms. *Theory into Practice, 31*, 132–141.

Morse, S. C. (1997). *Unschooled migrant youth: Characteristics and strategies to serve them.* Charleston, WV: Office of Educational Research and Improvement (ED). (ERIC Document Reproduction Service No. ED405158 1997-03-00). Retrieved June 9, 2008, from http://www.eric.ed.gov/contentdelivery/servlet/ERICServlet?accno=ED405158

Moskowitz, G. (1978). *Caring and sharing in the foreign language class: A sourcebook on humanistic techniques.* Rowley, MA: Newbury House.

National Center for Education Statistics. (2005). *National Institute of Statistical Sciences/Education Statistics Services Institute Task Force on Graduation, Completion, and Dropout Indicators: Final Report.* (NCES Publication No. 2005-105.) Washington, DC: U.S. Department of Education Institute of Education Sciences.

National Clearinghouse for English Language Acquisition & Language Instruction Educational Programs. (2005). *Ask NCELA No. 1: How many school-aged English language learners (ELLs) are there in the U.S.?* Office of English Language Acquisition. Retrieved January 8, 2008, from www.ncela.gwu.edu/expert/gaq/01leps.htm

National Governors' Association (2005). *Graduation counts: A report of the National Governors Association Task Force on state high school graduation data.* Retrieved January 10, 2008, from http://www.nga.org/Files/pdf/0507GRAD.PDF

National Institute of Child Health and Human Development (NICHD). (2000). *Report of the National Reading Panel. Teaching children to read: An evidence-based assessment of the scientific research literature on reading and its implications for reading instruction.* (NIH Publication No. 00-4769). Washington, DC: U.S. Department of Health and Human Services.

Nava, P., Hernandez, L., Rubalcava, A., & Palacios, E. (1995). *Empowering students and their families to succeed through innovative, diverse, and challenging educational programs.* Watsonville, CA: Pajaro Valley Unified School District; Office of Elementary and Secondary Education (ED). Washington, DC: Office of Migrant Education. ERIC Document Reproduction Service No. ED 462 208.

New York City Department of Education. (Summer, 2007). *New York City's English Language Learners: Demographics and Performance.* New York: Office of ELLs. Retrieved June 2008, from http://schools.nycenet.edu/offices/teachlearn/ell/DemoPerformanceFINAL_10_17.pdf

New York State Department of Education. *Elementary, Middle, Secondary and Continuing Education.* (n.d.). www.emsc.nysed.gov

Nieto, S. (2000). *Affirming diversity: The sociopolitical context of multicultural education.* Boston: Addison-Wesley.

Norton, B. (2000). *Identity and language learning: Gender, ethnicity and educational change.* Essex, UK: Pearson.

Nunan, D. (1991). *Language teaching methodology.* London: Prentice-Hall.

Oberg, K. (1960). Culture shock: adjustment to a new cultural environment. *Practical Anthropology, 7,* 177–182.

Olivos, E. M., & Quintana de Valladolid, C. E. (2005). Entre la espada y la pared: Critical educators, bilingual education, and education reform. *Journal of Latinos and Education, 4,* 11–293.

Olsen, L. (1997). *Made in America: Immigrant students in our public schools.* New York: New Press.

———. (2000). Learning English and learning America: Immigrants in the center of a story. *Theory into Practice, 39(4),* 196–202.

Olsen, L., & Jaramillo, A. (1999). *Turning the tides of exclusion: A guide for educators and advocates for immigrant students.* Oakland, CA: California Tomorrow.

Osterling, J. (2001). Waking the sleeping giant: engaging and capitalizing on the sociocultural strengths of the Latino community. *Bilingual Research Journal, 25,* 59–88.

Ovando, C. J., & Collier, V. P. (1998). *Bilingual and ESL classrooms: Teaching in multicultural contexts.* Boston: McGraw-Hill.

Ovando, D., Collier, V., & Combs, M. (2003). *Bilingual & ESL classrooms: Teaching in multicultural contexts* (3rd ed.). Boston: McGraw-Hill.

Papalia, A. (1976). *Learner-centered language teaching: Methods and materials.* Rowley, MA: Newbury House.

Papalia, A., & Zampogna, J. (1979). An experimental study on teachers' classroom behaviors and their effect on FL attrition. *The Modern Language Journal, 56,* 421–424.

Peregoy, S., & Boyle, O. (2008). *Reading, writing and learning in ESL: A resource book for teaching K–12 English learners* (5th ed.). Boston: Pearson/Allyn & Bacon.

Plevyak, L., & Heaston, A. (2001). The communications triangle of parents, school administrators, and teachers: A workshop model. *Education, 121,* 768–772.

Ramirez, J., & Merino, B. (1990). Classroom talk in English immersion, early-exit, and late-exit transitional bilingual education programs. In R. Jacobson & C. Faltis (Eds.), *Language distribution issues in bilingual schooling* (pp. 61–103). Clevedon, UK: Multilingual Matters.

Ramirez, J. D. (1992). Executive Summary. *Bilingual Research Journal, 16,* 1–62.

Richards, J. C., & Rogers, T. (2001). *Approaches and methods in language teaching.* Cambridge, UK: Cambridge University Press.

Robinson, D. H. (1998). Graphic organizers as aids to text learning. *Reading Research and Instruction, 37,* 85–105.

Rogers, C. (1966). To facilitate learning. In M. Provus (Ed), *Innovations for time to teach* (pp. 4–19). Washington, DC: National Education Association.

Rogers, C., & Freiberg, H. J. (1994). *Freedom to learn* (3rd ed.). New York: Macmillan/Merrill.

Rogoff, B., & Chavajay, P. (1995). What's become of research on the cultural basis of cognitive development? *American Psychologist, 50,* 859–877.

Rubenstein-Ávila, E. (2003). Facing reality: English language learners in middle school classes. *English Education, 35,* 122–136.

———. (2003–2004). Conversing with Miguel: An adolescent English language learner with later literacy development. *Journal of Adolescent & Adult Literacy, 47,* 290–301.

Ruiz-de-Velasco, J., & Fix, M. (2000). *Overlooked and underserved: Immigrant students in U.S. secondary schools.* Urban Institute. Retrieved March 10, 2008, from http://www.urban.org/JorgeRuizdeVelasco

Short, D. (2002a). Newcomer programs: An educational alternative for secondary immigrant students. *Education and Urban Society, 34,* 173–198.

———. (2002b). Language learning in sheltered social studies classes. *TESOL Quarterly, 11,* 18–24.

Slavin, R. (1995). *Cooperative learning: Theory, research, and practice* (2ⁿᵈ ed.). Boston: Allyn & Bacon.

Slavin R., & Madden, N. (2001). *One million children.* Thousand Oaks, CA: Corwin Press.

Stoller, F. (2002). Project work: A means to promote language and content. In J. C. Richards & W. A. Renandya (Eds.), *Methodology in language teaching* (pp. 107–119). Cambridge, UK: Cambridge University Press.

Suarez-Orozco, M. (1989). *Central American refugees and U.S. high schools: A psychological study of motivation and achievement.* Stanford, CA: Stanford University Press.

Tartir, S. (2007). *Immigration and America's schools: Introduction to the issues.* Washington, DC: National Clearinghouse for English Language Acquisition. Retrieved May 19, 2008, from http://www.ncela.gwu.edu/resabout/literacy

Tienda, M., & Mitchell, F. (Eds.). (2006). *Multiple origins, uncertain destinies: Hispanics and the American future.* Washington, DC: The National Academies Press.

Triandis, H. C. (1995). *Individualism and collectivism.* Boulder, CO: Westview Press.

Trueba, H., Jacobs, L., & Kirton, E. (1990). *Cultural conflict and adaptation: The case of Hmong children in American society.* New York: Falmer Press.

Trumball, E., Rothstein-Fisch, C., Greenfield, P., & Quiroz, B. (2001). *Bridging cultures between home and school: A guide for teachers.* Mahwah, NJ: Lawrence Erlbaum.

Tulviste, P. (1991). *The cultural-historical development of verbal thinking.* (M.J. Hall, Trans.). Comack, NY: Nova Science.

Valdes, G. (2001). *Learning and not learning English: Latino students in American schools.* New York: Teachers College Press.

Valenzuela, A. (1999). *Subtractive schooling: U.S.-Mexican youth and the politics of caring.* New York: State University of New York Press.

Valenzuela, A., Fuller, E., & Vasquez-Heilig. (2006). The disappearance of high school English language learners from Texas high schools. *Williams Institute Journal, 1,* 170–200.

Walsh, C. (1999). *Enabling academic success for secondary students with limited formal schooling: A Study of the Haitian literacy program at Hyde Park High School in Boston.* Brown University: LAB.

Watts-Taffe, S., & Truscott, D. (2000). Using what we know about language and literacy development for ESL students in the mainstream classroom. *Language Arts, 77,* 258–265.

Vygotsky, L. (1978). *Mind in society: The development of higher psychological processes.* Cambridge, MA: Harvard University Press.

Wilson, B. G., & Cole, P. (1991). A review of cognitive teaching models. *Educational Technology Research & Development, 39,* 47–64.

Xu, S. H. (2003). Literacy-related play with an intergeneration of students' "funds of knowledge."
    International Journal of Social Education, 18, 9–16.

Zhou, M., & Bankston, C. (2000). The biculturation of the Vietnamese student. *ERIC Clearinghouse on
    Urban Education, 152,* 1–7.

Index